THE SHOOTING ~~SCRIPT~~
UNITED 93

Screenplay and commentary by
Paul Greengrass

NHB Shooting Scripts
NICK HERN BOOKS • LONDON
www.nickhernbooks.co.uk

Screenplay, Motion Picture Artwork, and Photography ™ & © 2006 Universal Studios. All rights reserved.

Initial Treatment copyright © 2006 Paul Greengrass.
All rights reserved. Used by permission.

This book first published in Great Britain in 2006 as an original paperback
by Nick Hern Books Ltd, The Glasshouse, 49A Goldhawk Road, London W12 8QP,
by arrangement with Newmarket Press, New York.

A CIP catalogue record of this book is available from the British Library.

ISBN-13 978-1-85459-983-4
ISBN-10 1-85459-983-6

This book may not be reproduced in whole or in part in any form
without written permission of the publisher.

Manufactured in the United States of America.

THE NHB SHOOTING SCRIPT SERIES

The Actors
Adaptation
A Beautiful Mind
Big Fish
Capote
Cinderella Man
Erin Brockovich
Eternal Sunshine of the Spotless Mind
The Good Shepherd
Gosford Park
I Went Down
The Ice Storm
In Good Company
Saltwater
The Shawshank Redemption
The Squid and the Whale
The Truman Show

For information on forthcoming titles, please contact the publisher:
Nick Hern Books, The Glasshouse, 49A Goldhawk Road, London W12 8QP
e-mail: info@nickhernbooks.demon.co.uk

CONTENTS

Initial Treatment	v
The Shooting Script	1
Stills	*following page 86*
Q & A with Paul Greengrass	87
About the Production	91
"9/11 Live" by Michael Bronner	105
Film Reviews	
Martin Amis	137
Peter Bradshaw	142
David Denby	145
Stephen King	148
United Airlines Flight 93's Crew and Passengers	152
About the Flight 93 National Memorial	153
Cast and Crew Credits	155
About the Writer/Director	165

Dedicated to the memory of the passengers and crew
of United 93, and to their families

INITIAL TREATMENT

PAUL GREENGRASS

Editor's Note: Paul Greengrass wrote this initial treatment in July 2005, expressing why he wanted to make a film about 9/11, which led to his making the movie that released on April 28, 2006.

This twenty-one-page treatment included a time-coded, scene-by-scene plot of the flight of United 93 that morning of 9/11 as viewed by those in the flight towers and military centers as well as those aboard the plane itself. This initial treatment was used to pitch the project, and a production deal was completed by the summer of 2005. Principal photography began in mid-November 2005 at Pinewood Studios in England.

More on this production process can be found later in this volume.

What Does It Mean? (On United 93)

That's the question we ask ourselves over and over again. Does it mean war without end? The onset of a new fascism. A shadow over all of our lives.

Or is it instead a chance to renew our vows of patriotism? Of heroism. A chance to write a burnished page in history.

Perhaps it's a wake-up call. An event so calamitous that it forces us to acknowledge the fire raging outside. Makes us engage with the world. Drain the swamp.

Or was it just a chance event? Something terrible and unrepeatable that lacks meaning beyond itself. We mourn, remember the victims, but draw no lasting conclusions.

I doubt it.

I think we all know that somehow, in some way, it changed things in our lifetime forever.

There's lots of ways to find meaning in the events of 9/11, especially as we move toward next year's fifth anniversary.

Television can convey events as they happen. A reporter can write history's rough first draft. Historians can widen the time frame and give us context. Politicians can seek to ride the waves of emotion. The best of them can lead us, too. Religious leaders divine spiritual meanings and give us comfort. There are many ways…

Well, I make films and I believe they have a small part to play, too. And I also believe that sometimes, if you look clearly and unflinchingly at a single event, you can find in its shape something precious, something much larger than the event itself…the DNA of our times.

Hence a film about Flight 93.

Here is the perfect metaphor of our times.

Think of the plane—a beautiful state-of-the-art Boeing 757. Sleek contours, advanced avionics, the awesome power of those Rolls-Royce engines. A silver-skinned bird able to defy gravity and vault across time and space at unbelievable speed. It is truly the finest creation of our Western civilization—a thing of beauty, power, and poetry. But before it took off that morning into the clear blue sky it needed, just as we all need…

Gasoline. Thousands and thousands of greedy, guzzling gallons of gasoline.

Then think of the passengers—rising to alarm clocks, throwing on their branded clothes, racing in cars, grabbing Starbucks coffee and newspapers, hurrying to catch that plane. Each with private loves and lives, each meeting at the check-in and leaving those lives behind. There was nothing special about them. They could have been me. They could have been you.

And they gathered together in that gas-guzzling silver metal tube packed full of the most advanced technology our world can provide and sealed themselves in hermetically. Literally sealed themselves away from the rest of the world, as the pilot and stewardesses conducted those strange secular safety rituals that comfort us in our outrageous modernity.

They thought they were safe. They were tragically blind. Appallingly unlucky. Because on this day, September 11, 2001, the world out there, viewed dimly in the casually glanced-at pages of newspapers, or in occasional television fragments…the world of anarchy and poverty and anger and resentment…was not far away at all.

It was sitting in four first-class seats right next to them.

And then imagine the hijackers.

Three uneducated Saudis, led by a wealthy Lebanese reformed playboy. Think of their prayers, the intensity of the beliefs that drove them to strike in a suicide mission at the heart of America's power. They were terrifyingly devout killers. But of course they were blind too—to humanity, to decency, to pity—driven as they were by deeply irrational religious hate.

Above all, of course, they were real. And as we weigh the crucial issues before us today—where do we go from here, how do we deal with the post-9/11 world? —we should never forget that central fact. The threat is real. Or so it seems to me.

And the question asked of the passengers on Flight 93, the terrible, terrible dilemma they faced, is the same question we have been facing ever since: Do we hope this all turns out okay, or do we fight back? Do we strike at them before they strike at us? And what will be the consequences if we do?

This is why, I believe, the events on that plane continue to hold such immense power over us….for although we can only dimly understand the shape of what went on during that ninety-minute flight, we can know enough—from the two dozen phone calls, from the thirty minutes of cockpit voice recordings—to know that at some level it distills and symbolizes everything that we face today.

The hermetically sealed world disrupted by a savage and violent act. The passengers herded to the back of the plane. The hijackers turning the plane round and setting course for Washington. The passengers searching for intelligence as to what was happening to them, reaching out to the authorities on the ground and to loved ones via air phone, only to discover that they were caught in some vast suicidal plot.

Then, as Flight 93 begins to close in on the Capitol, the rational debate that we know the passengers conducted amidst the terror: Do we strike back and risk destruction, or hope for the best and risk destruction? And then, even more extraordinarily, the passengers vote, whilst in the cockpit there are only prayers and suicidal devotion.

And then the fight back. The struggle for the controls of the plane—a struggle that went on and on and on for perhaps seven minutes. Until finally the plane crashes….

That final image haunts me, draws me grimly into its embrace—a physical struggle for the controls of a gasoline-fueled twenty-first-century flying machine between a band of suicidal religious fanatics and a group of innocents drawn at random from amongst us all.

I think of it often. It's the struggle for our world today.

United 93

Written by
Paul Greengrass

FINAL SHOOTING SCRIPT

FLIGHT 93

INT. 4x4. KANDAHAR. DAY

A traveling POV - dusty streets, shanty houses, open sewers. Groups of men standing, women carrying heavy loads, children scratching in shadows. We could be anywhere – Africa, the Middle East, South America.

In fact we're in Kandahar, Afghanistan.

EXT. SLUMS. KANDAHAR. DAY

A convoy of vehicles – a red Toyota leading a black 4x4 with tinted windows and a white station wagon behind – sweeping through the slums towards their destination. Scarcely anyone looks up as they pass by.

EXT. AL MATAR COMPLEX. DAY

The convoy approaches a compound on the outskirts of town. White walls, barbed wire, sentry towers. Obvious signs of armed security outside. This is the Al Matar complex, Osama Bin Laden's principal base of operations in Afghanistan.

Bring up the date: April 17th 1999

We sweep through into the courtyard. The vehicles slow to a halt. Out steps a man in a faded canvas suit carrying a briefcase. His name is Khaled Sheikh Mohammed. He has been an active international terrorist for almost half of his 38 years.

From a distance we watch as he goes inside. Through windows we see him walk down a hallway. He waits momentarily outside a door. It opens. As he goes in we catch a glimpse – no more – of a tall imposing figure in a white shirt and combat tunic.

The door closes and we cut to:

EXT. NEW YORK. DAWN

Dawn breaking over the New York skyline.

And we bring up the date: September 11th 2001.

0530

EXT. NEWARK AIRPORT

In the half-light we make out rows and rows of gleaming humming silver birds.

Newark is gearing up for a busy September day.

In the distance we see Newark tower.

INT. NEWARK TOWER. CONTINUOUS

Radio chatter. Controllers huddle over screens, checking in with other centers. Things are running smoothly at Newark Airport Tower.

One small cog in the vast US air traffic system.

EXT. APPROACH ROAD. HERNDON CENTER

Ben Sliney pulls in to his parking space at the FAA's National Air Traffic Command Center.

He turns off the engine and pauses looking out at the building in front.

As newly appointed FAA National Operations Manager, today he will be in charge of the entire US air traffic system.

He gathers his things and heads for the entrance.

INT. HERNDON CENTER FOYER

Sliney signs in. Jokes with a receptionist about his promotion as he is handed a new security pass. Gets a coffee.

He nods at familiar faces along the corridors, taking the banter as he goes.

He reaches the door to the Operations Center and goes in.

INT. OPERATIONS CENTER. HERNDON

It's a big, open room – 100 feet wide, 50 feet deep, very high ceilings. There are 7 tiers of console clusters, with 7 large projection screens (about 10'x12') covering the long, lower wall.

On the main shifts, there are around 50 people present – 30 ATC specialists and supervisors arrayed in consoles, plus 20 other airline and military liaison and communications staff divided by region and focus (East, West, Severe Weather etc)

As Sliney walks the line of controllers he gets his first briefing of the day from the midnight supervisor at the watch desk, located on the floor bottom-right and decked out with weather monitors, a "status board" showing ground delays, ground stops, etc. The supervisor is off shift, and eager to go. He keeps it short and sweet.

SUPERVISOR
A little weather out west. Nothing to worry about. No ground stops. Delays minimal.

SLINEY
Anything I should know about?

SUPERVISOR
The President is travelling today. He's in Florida. We've got restrictions in place until 10:30 a.m, and that's it.

SLINEY
And that's it?

SUPERVISOR
That's it. It's all yours Ben.

The midnight supervisor exits, leaving Sliney looking up at the massive screen high on the wall. Watches the electronic dots building across North America in perfect synchronicity. Soon there will be almost 5000 planes aloft.

"Clockwork" Sliney thinks to himself. A thing of beauty.

0530   **INT. DAYS INN. NEWARK AIRPORT**

In a hotel room near to the airport two men are praying.

Bent prostrate on the floor. Abject. Devotional. These are Saeed al Ghamdi and Ahmed al Nami.

They recite passages from the Koran about forgiveness and martyrdom - the two Suras, Al Tawba 'Repentance' and Al Anfa 'The spoils of war.'

> O Allah! If this is indeed
> The Truth from Thee,
> Rain down on us a shower of stones from the sky,
> Or send us a grievous Penalty

The modern world reduced to medieval simplicities.

INT. ANOTHER HOTEL. NEWARK AIRPORT

An early morning alarm wakes United Airlines pilot Jason Dahl. He showers and puts on his uniform half watching the news and weather.

Dahl has altered his schedule so that he can see his mother in San Jose, California and be back at the weekend to celebrate his wedding anniversary.

Today he will fly United Airlines Flight 93.

0545   **INT. DAYS INN. NEWARK AIRPORT**

In another room two more young men are concluding their morning prayers. These are Ahmad al Haznawi and Ziad Jarrah, leader of the Flight 93 operation.

They begin to shave all excess hair and wash their bodies. They dry and perfume. They dress, following an intense and particular ritual, the details of which were later discovered in Mohammed Atta's luggage.

> Vow to accept death, renew admonition, shave the extra hair on the body, perfume yourself, and ritually wash yourself.
>
> Completely forget something called 'this life'. The time for play is over and the serious time is upon us.

Let your breast be filled with gladness, for there is nothing between you and your wedding but mere seconds.

INT. MARRIOTT. NEWARK AIRPORT

Flight attendant Sandra Bradshaw shuts off the showerhead and grabs for a towel in the small en suite bathroom of her shared hotel room.

Other stewardesses are asleep. Some on the bed, some on the floor. Uniforms hang throughout, draped on chairs and curtain rails.

Bradshaw blow-dries her hair and dresses in the mirror.

As she grabs her trolley case from the corner a colleague stirs.

STEWARDESS
Sandy? You gone already?

BRADSHAW
Yeah - I'm on 93 to San Fran.

Bradshaw creeps out of the room and closes the door.

INT. THE DAYS INN. NEWARK AIRPORT

Haznawi and Jarrah begin to prepare their luggage.

Mundane items at first - clothes, shoes, papers etc.

Then more curious items, children's clay, red tape, a roll of wire, a battery, a canister of pepper spray, a red bandanna and lastly…

A 3.5-inch ceramic knife.

Haznawi doesn't pack this, but tucks it into his belt. No need to conceal what is perfectly legal after all.

They leave the room.

0600   ### INT. TAXI. TOWARDS NEWARK AIRPORT.

A businessman is on the move – leaving a voice mail message for his boss. Hey, good news there's room on an earlier flight. I'll make the meeting.

He calls the car company.

> BURNETT
> Yeah reference 2020. Thomas Burnett. I'm taking the earlier flight. United 93. I'll need a car to meet me in San Francisco.

Now he calls his secretary to leave word about his change of itinerary.

> BURNETT
> Hi, it's me. Change of plan. I'm in at ten so check the car, I'm going straight to the eleven o'clock.

He's focussed, accurate, decisive – parsing hours into minutes, minutes into seconds. Making his time count. No wonder Thomas Burnett is one of America's leading businessmen under 40.

Today he too will fly Flight 93.

0645   **EXT/INT. DAYS INN. NEWARK AIRPORT**

Al Ghamdi and Al Nami leave their rooms.

Down the monotonous corridors and out into the lobby.

INT. TAXI TOWARDS NEWARK AIRPORT

Jason Dahl makes his way to the airport.

INT. SHUTTLEBUS.

Sandra Bradshaw is on the move too. Hurriedly putting on lipstick as the bus pulls into the approach road to the airport.

EXT. DAYS INN. NEWARK AIRPORT

Jarrah collects his car from the lot. Pulls the car round to reception.

See Haznawi waiting for the others.

As we see Jarah's face clearly for the first time, we wonder if there is any moment of doubt or hesitation, pity or compassion.

Suddenly he flips open his cell phone and dials a number. As it answers he speaks six words in Arabic quickly.

>   JARRAH
> I love you. I love you.

He rings off.

Haznawi, Al Ghamdi and Al Nami walk out to meet Jarrah.

The car pulls away.

0700 **INT /EXT. TAXI. NEWARK AIRPORT**

Flight 93 pilot Jason Dahl pulls up outside the airport and enters the Terminal building.

INT. TERMINAL BUILDING. NEWARK AIRPORT

Inside the Terminal Building "Good morning America" flickers on airport televisions throughout the hall.

Dahl descends a flight of stairs into the lower level.

INT. UNITED AIRLINES OPERATIONS CENTRE

Jason Dahl enters the United Airlines' Operations Center through an unlocked door.

He walks down the hall to a hatch. Inside a flight office rep hands him paperwork. Dahl takes it, checks his "NOTAMs" (Notice to Airmen) in his mailbox, which tell pilots of any important changes or irregularities.

Then meets Leroy Homer, his First Officer for the day. They have never flown together before.

They sit with other pilot teams at a long, slanted desktop in the cramped pilots area, going over the paper work. Yesterday's thunderstorms have blown out. But Dahl is concerned about fuel and calls up the dispatcher. It's the daily haggling of every pilot's life. The airlines give the minimum. The pilots always want more.

> DAHL
> Hey, this is Jason Dahl flying Flight 93 to San Fran. I'm a little concerned about the fuel. I'd like to add a couple thousand because there's lo viz in San Fran.

After a bit of to and fro Dahl gets the fuel he needs. He signs his paperwork and gives a carbon copy to the flight office rep on the other side of the desk. The rep enters the changes into the computer.

Dahl and Homer head out to the airplane.

INT. GATE 17

Dahl and Homer walk past the passenger waiting area and down the jetway to the plane.

INT. FLIGHT 93

Dahl settles in as Homer dumps his bag and walks back onto the jetway, out the side door and down some steps.

EXT. GATE 17. TARMAC

We follow Homer out into the open air and there it is, for the first time -a magnificent Boeing 757-200.. A thing of power and delicacy. A beautiful man-made silver bird.

This is Flight 93.

INT. COCKPIT FLIGHT 93

Dahl settles into his seat and begins his pre-flight checklist, moving across the aircraft's bewildering array of switches, gauges and computers.

It's wondrous complexity.

EXT. FLIGHT 93

Homer waves to a maintenance worker as he gets out of a fuel truck.

Watches as he connects a fuel pipe to the wing.

As Homer begins his inspection, the fuel workers open the hydrant's valve with a blast of compressed air.

Gauges on the wing leap to life as the fuel rushes into the planes tanks at 100 psi .

INT. FUEL PIPE VFX

We follow the Kerosene as it gushes, through a filtration system and up the pipes into the plane, filling its vast tanks, with the precious liquid.

Flight 93 is a greedy, greedy bird.

EXT. NEWARK TERMINAL.

The four hijackers park in the Terminal car park and walk towards the Terminal Building. They pass other passengers arriving to board United Airlines 93.

Passenger Ed Felt walks towards the terminal, a briefcase in hand, a newspaper under his arm.

Passenger Georgine Corrigan says goodbye to her brother. She organizes her three suitcases with a skycap, a carry-on full of her jewelry hanging from the crook of her arm.

Passenger Mark Rothenberg crushes out one last cigarette as he exits his taxi and goes towards the Terminal doors.

INT. UNITED AIRLINES DOMICILE

We follow Sandra Bradshaw as she moves through the terminal building and enters the domicile through an unmarked door in the airport's innards. She punches in a security code, and enters United's flight-attendant operations center.

At the counter she scribbles her initials by her name on what United calls the FLT LOF; the line of flight. She is now officially on duty. She pours a coffee and sits down at the meeting table.

Senior Flight Attendant Deborah Welsh comes over and greets Bradshaw and two other attendants –CeeCee Lyles and Lorraine Bay - as they gather at a table.

Wanda Green is the last to arrive as always.

                    GREEN
        Sorry guys – traffic.

She hangs up her coat and finds a place at the table.

The group is complete.

They run through the flight. First they allocate roles. Welsh is the purser - the No1. She will be working first class, Green and Bay up front in coach, Lyles and Bradshaw at the back of the plane.

Given Bradshaw's seniority she would usually work up front, but she doesn't mind. Today she's just happy to be flying and part of a team.

Before leaving for the gate, they check over the passenger manifest. The flight will be less than half full.

0700   **EXT/ INT. NEWARK TERMINAL BUILDING.**

The four hijackers enter the Terminal building.

Al Nami and Al Ghamdi first. Then Haznawi. Jarrah hangs back waiting.

As they move through the concourse they filter out the banal chatter that surrounds them.

Briefcases, cell phones, lovers farewells - this is not their world. It is the world of the *Kufr* - the unbeliever.

Al Nami passes Linda Gronlund, an Environmental Compliance Manager, as she hauls her luggage down the walkway with boyfriend, Joseph DeLuca.

Al Ghamdi passes student Nicole Miller who is saying goodbye to her friend Ryan Brown after spending some time together in New York.

Haznawi looks back as Donald Greene, a 52 year-old vice president of the Safe Flight Instrument Corporation passes him.

Still Jarrah is watching.

INT. LIMO PULLING UP TO TERMINAL BUILDING

Now Thomas Burnett is arriving too.

EXT. CONCOURSE TERMINAL BUILDING

Burnett still on the phone, tips the driver and steps out towards the concourse, through the jam of traffic and exhaust fumes. Newark is hotting up. It's rush hour.

He walks into the terminal.

EXT. TARMAC. GATE 17

As the fuel flows, Homer continues to inspect the plane.

The tail fin, the wings tips, the huge turbo fan Pratt & Whitney engines.

The maintenance worker, checks the dials and shuts off the fuel hose. Fueling is complete.

The maintenance worker prints out a receipt for the fuel.

0715   ### INT. AIRCRAFT JETWAY/CABIN. FLIGHT 93.

Sandra Bradshaw and the other stewardesses now head down the jetway into the cabin.

When she enters, she goes to the back of the plane to carry out her safety checks.

She and CeeCee Lyles work quickly and efficiently. They are friends and have flown together before.

They look over their jump seats to make sure life vests and flashlights are in place, then examine the oxygen bottles and pressure gauges.

Deborah Welsh checks the video system and makes sure the cockpit key is hidden in its secret place in the galley. She then goes into the cabin to introduce herself to the captain.

INT COCKPIT. FLIGHT 93

Dahl greets Welsh and gives her the headlines. There may be a little chop over the Rockies; flight time is five hours forty. He'd like to eat about an hour in.

They establish the secret knock that will allow her to gain access to the cabin.

"Three and one." He tells her.

As Welsh leaves the cabin, the maintenance worker enters and asks Dahl to sign for the fuel.

Dahl signs for 48,700 pounds of Kerosene.

It's getting busy.

0715

EXT. AIRCRAFT FLIGHT 93

Meanwhile, co-pilot Leroy Homer is completing his inspection of the outside of the plane.

He checks tire pressure, looks inside the engines, radios Dahl and asks him to turn on the external lights to check they're working.

Up close, at ground level we get a sense of the scale of this awesome machine.

Checks complete Homer bounds up the jetway to join Dahl in the cockpit.

0715
(0705)

INT.TERMINAL BUILDING.NEWARK AIRPORT

Al Ghamdi and Al Nami check in at a United Airlines desk.

Al Nami puts two bags onto the conveyor belt.

                    AGENT
         You traveling alone today, sir?

Al Nami nods. His English is almost non-existent.

                    AGENT
         Did you pack these bags yourself?

Another nod.
                    AGENT
         Did anyone give you anything to take on the airplane?

A shake of the head.

We begin to have an unnerving sense of their utter disengagement from the polite rituals that attend our 21st century lives.

Al Ghamdi steps up now, glancing across to Haznawi who has taken up position at a desk further down.

Haznawi checks one bag.

The Computer Assisted Passenger Pre-screening System selects him through risk algorithm calculation. The ticket agent puts a special tag on his checked luggage, then processes his check in.

Haznawi's knife is visible in his belt, hilt up and clear to see.

Jarrah is watching on from the seated area near the entrance.

Sees Al Nami and Al Ghamdi move away from check-in.

Then Haznawi soon after.

As he sees his younger accomplices disappear down the escalators towards security, Jarrah steps up to United's first class desk and checks in.

They are over the first hurdle.

INT. SECURITY AREA

We follow Jarrah as he travels towards security, past fellow passengers, Louis Nacke and Japanese student Toshiya Kuge.

Again Jarrah hangs back, watching as al Ghamdi and al Nami , arrive at the security checkpoint, run by United Airlines and operated under contract by Argenbright Security.

They pass through without event.

Haznawi is a little further back. He approaches the checkpoint, laying his hand luggage on the conveyor belt.

INT .WALKWAY

Al Nami and Al Ghamdi walk towards Gate 17 moving through lines of commuters.

INT. SECURITY AREA

Haznawi empties his loose change into a small plastic bowl before passing into the metal detector.

Still his knife is visible, hilt up. No one confiscates the weapon.

The security screener looks at his bag as it crosses through the x-ray.

We pick out the roll of wire, the battery, a pepper-spray canister, duct tape.

All innocuous items.

In the background, Jarrah watches on.

Haznawi waits.

INT. GATE 17

Al Nami and Al Ghamdi arrive at the gate now.

They look around at their fellow travellers at Gate 17.

The two hijackers sit down side by side in between Christian Adams and Deora Bodley.

Nearby, Jeremy Glick sets down his bag down and takes a seat opposite Alan Beaven.

INT. SECURITY AREA

Haznawi collects his loose change from the bowl, and retrieves his bag.

He is through.

Todd Beamer, who is traveling to the West Coast for a business meeting, steps up to the metal detector.

Behind him Colleen Fraser places her bag on the conveyor belt.

With Haznawi through Jarrah proceeds towards the checkpoint joining another line between Donald and Jean Peterson, and Christine Snyder.

INT. WALKWAY ENTRANCE

Haznawi hovers, watching to see if Jarrah clears security.

Jane Folger, Patricia Cushing and John Talignani, pass him by, oblivious to the deadly choreography that is playing out before them.

Jarrah clears too - without a flicker of anxiety.

One glance from Jarrah and Haznawi is on the move.

They are through.

INT. WALKWAY

Haznawi and Jarrah -still separate- make their way down the long wide central corridor past wall advertisements with banal tag lines.

Through their eyes we see our world in a very different light- frivolous, sexualized, and superficial.

Above all unsuspecting.

INT. CAR. TRAVELLING.

Mark Bingham is running late. A six foot four former rugby champion at the University of California at Berkeley, Bingham runs a public relations firm in San Francisco with a branch in New York.

Its touch and go as to whether he will make it onto his flight this morning.

He spies the twin towers of the World Trade Center from the passenger seat of his friend Mark Hall's Chevy Beretta, as they speed towards Newark Airport.

                MARK BINGHAM
Hey, look-New York.

0740   **INT GATE 17**

The lounge is filling. Kristin White Gould arrives, then Lauren Grandcolas, and Richard Guadagno.

The last of the hijackers arrive too, assimilating themselves effortlessly within the humdrum commuter scene.

Haznawi, hovers for a while then sits a couple of seats away from Mark Rothenberg.

Jarrah too, walks to the window passing Waleska Martinez and Marion Britton.

He sits down and, surveys the gathering crowd.

Nervous flyers gather their thoughts. Experienced commuter travelers work their palm pilots.

And still the passengers arrive - Andrew Garcia, William Cashman, Honor Elizabeth Wainio.

There are last minute phone calls, both business and personal.

Nicole Miller makes a call to Ryan Brown - a brief farewell.

Mickey Rothenberg calls a business associate with last minute details about their meeting.

Linda Gronlund chats with her sister. Linda and her boyfriend Joseph Deluca are on heading for the west coast.

Thomas Burnett arrives too. As a first class passenger he checks in at the gate, and then looks for a seat.

He strolls past Hilda Marcin, Patrick 'Joe' Driscoll and Jeremy Glick who is trying to call home.

> GLICK
> Tell her I love her and I'll call when I get to San Francisco.

Burnett takes a seat next to Jarrah. Makes a call, oblivious to the intense young man sitting next to him, whose thoughts are far away.

> Know the plane well from every angle. Anticipate the reaction or the resistance of the enemy.
>
> You must make your knife sharp and you must not discomfort your animal during the slaughter.

Jarrah looks at his watch and flips open his cell. He gets up and moves to a quiet corner. Dials a number. A moments hesitation.

He speaks quickly in Arabic.

> JARRAH
> We are ready.

Just then ground staff at gate 17 make the first call for Flight 93.

0741 **INT. FLIGHT 93**

In the cockpit pilot Jason Dahl powers up the plane's ground electrical system.

The passengers begin to board the plane.

Flight attendants Lorraine Bay and Wanda Green stand at the doorway, ushering the ten passengers in first class down the aisle to their left and the twenty-seven in coach down to their right, towards Sandra Bradshaw.

In total there are 44 people, 37 passengers, 2 pilots, 5 flight attendants, in amongst them - 4 hijackers.

The hijackers sit in first class, which consists of six rows each with three seats. Jarrah is in seat 1B, closest to the cockpit; al Nami is in 3C; al Ghamdi in 3D and al Haznawi in 6B.

Later the FBI would discover the 9/11 operation's leader Mohammad Atta's instruction manual in a car left at Boston Airport.

> In the plane as soon as you get on, you should pray to God…
>
> As soon as you board the aeroplane and have taken your seat, remember that which you were told earlier and devote yourself to remember God.
>
> God says that when you are surrounded by several non-believers, you must sit quietly and remember that God will make victory possible.

Senior stewardess Deborah Welsh interrupts their prayers. Offers them newspapers and refreshments. The hijackers again decline monosyllabically.

Now we understand. Their disengagement is total. Lethal.

0750   **EXT. CONCOURSE. NEWARK AIRPORT**

Hall's Chevy Beretta pulls up at the United terminal. Bingham gives him a hug and rushes inside. He's late for boarding.

INT. WALKWAY. NEWARK AIRPORT

Bingham sprints up the central corridor to Gate 17.

INT. GATE 17. NEWARK AIRPORT

He checks in, and dashes down the jetway.

INT. CABIN. FLIGHT 93

He steps up just as the door is about to be closed. He is the last person to board the plane takes seat 4D in first class, just behind Al Ghamdi and across the aisle from Thomas Burnett.

The cabin crew close the doors and pull the locking mechanism across.

INT. DOOR LOCKING MECHANISM VFX

Inside the locking mechanism the bolt engages and locks.

Those aboard Flight 93 are sealed in.

Safe from the dangers of a turbulent world.

INT. HERNDON COMMAND CENTER

Back at the National Air Traffic Command Center, Controller Ben Sliney makes his way across the floor, back to his desk.

He's got the regular once every two hour tele-conference with all Centers, TRACONs, major airlines, etc., called the "spit" (for Special Planning Telcon).

When he gets on the line there's a lot of banter for the new guy on the bridge. It's a buddy world air traffic control, bullish but trusting.

> COLLEAGUE
> See the thing is Ben, perfection cannot be improved.

> SLINEY
> You watch me.

0759   ### EXT. BOSTON LOGAN AIRPORT TOWER

Six hundred miles to the north, a huge gas laden American Airlines 767 bound for Los Angeles, taxis then pauses at the foot of a runway.

> TOWER
> American 11, this is Boston Logan Tower, you are cleared for take off.

> AMERICAN 11
> Roger that.

0800   **EXT. BOSTON LOGAN AIRPORT**

American 11 thunders down the runway and into the air.

0801   **INT. BOSTON CENTER**

An extreme close up of American 11's transponder signal as it refreshes across the radar screen.

Radio traffic fades in and out describing it's route as it passes from Logan Tower.

To Terminal Approach.

And eventually out into Boston Center airspace.

We pull out to see a Boston Center Controller Pete Zalewski seated in front of a broad, square-screened radar scope in one of Boston Center's five U-shaped radar areas.

                    ZALEWSKI
    American 11 you are with Boston Center on channel 3.

                    AMERICAN 11
    Roger. Boston Center. American 11.

Zalewski takes another routine flight on to his screen.

INT NEWARK TOWER

Inside Newark Tower, Controller Callahan listens to a call for push back from pilot Jason Dahl aboard UA93.

                    UNITED 93
    This is United 93, gate 17. We're ready for push-back.

                    TOWER
    United 93, You're clear to push.

EXT. TARMAC. GATE 17

A hard wired ground guy signals to the cockpit.

0801   **INT COCKPIT FLIGHT 93**

Jason Dahl and co pilot LeRoy Homer, prepare for push back.

> CAPT
> Okay. We're clear to push. Brakes set.

> GROUND GUY
> Release brakes.

> CAPT
> Breaks released. Clear to push.

The plane rolls backwards, comes to a halt.

> GROUND GUY
> Set brakes. Clear to start engines.

> CAPT
> Brakes set. Pressure normal. Clear to start, start number two.

> GROUND GUY
> Toe bar's disconnected. Can I disconnect the headset?

> CAPT
> Clear to disconnect the headset. We'll watch for your salute. Have a good day.

EXT. TARMAC GATE 17

The Ground guy gives the all clear with a brief salute. Dahl flashes the taxi lights to confirm.

INT. NEWARK TOWER

Callahan directs Flight 93 to the taxiway.

> CAPT
> Newark Ground, this is United 93, taxiway Romeo Alpha, ready for taxi.

> TOWER
> Roger, United 93. Taxi to runway Two-Two Right Bravo.

INT. CABIN FLIGHT 93

In the cabin Sandy Bradshaw and CeeCee Lyles begin the safety procedures.

> WELSH
> Ladies and Gentlemen on behalf of Captain Jason Dahl I would like to welcome you onboard this non-stop flight to San Francisco.

Some passengers - not many – watch.

> WELSH
> At this time as the doors have now been closed I would ask you to please put your tray tables up and your seats back in the upright position and switch off all cellular phones and other electrical devices.

Most passengers are reading. Newspapers. Magazines. The news is humdrum, domestic, unaware.

Tucked away on international pages we glimpse stories from a troubled world. War, struggle, poverty, hunger.

Some passengers talk. Some make clear in their body language to the person next to them that they don't wish to engage.

In first class Burnett is still on the phone. Relentlessly focused on the business of the day. He wraps up the call.

Across the way, Bingham calls Hall who is now driving home.

> BINGHAM
> Thanks for driving me. I made the plane. I'm in first class, drinking a glass of orange juice.

He turns off his phone also.

In seat 1B, Jarrah, sits deep in prayer, following Atta's instructions.

> When the aeroplane moves, as soon as it starts to move slowly start praying the prayers of travelling Muslims, because you travel in order to meet God and to enjoy the journey.

Al Nami and Al Ghamdi in 3C and 3D, and Haznawi 6B are doing the same.

An intense silent commune.

INT. COCKPIT FLIGHT 93

In the cockpit Jason Dahl and Leroy Homer steer the plane out onto the taxiway.

> DAHL
> Give me flaps 5 when you're ready.

Homer begins the take-off check-list, re-checking flaps, weight and balance. United faxes them a final weight figure, which they check against what's entered into the computer.

> TOWER
> United 93, monitor tower on one-eighteen-three.

> DAHL
> One-eighteen-three, Roger.

The plane is now in the system.

0813   **INT BOSTON ATC**

Controller Pete Zalewski is still handling American 11 at his screen as it tracks out west. He's been working the morning shift since 7am.

As a gay man with a business degree, he's probably in the minority among controllers, but he loves the intensity and is pushing 25 years on the job. By all accounts, he's good at it. Today he will have to be.

> BOSTON
> American 11 turn twenty degrees right.

> FLIGHT 11
> Twenty right, American 11.

16 seconds later Zalewski instructs American 11 to climb to 35000 feet.

There's no response.

He repeats the command.

> ZALEWSKI
> American 11 – Boston Center, How do you hear…?
> American 11 – Boston Center… American 11 - Boston Center..

Still no response.

Zalewski turns to the controller next to him – Greg Taccini, who has just handed American 11 off to Zalewski.

> ZALEWSKI
> Greg, can you check and see if you have American 11 back on your frequency? I'm not getting him.

> TACINNI
> American 11 – Boston Center…American 11 – Boston Center, how do you hear…?

Nothing.

Zalewski switches to emergency frequency to try to reach the pilot.

No reply.

That's odd, thinks Zalewski.

American 11 is now heading out of his air space, on to another controllers screen. He hands off the flight with a few strokes of the keyboard.

Zalewski radios across to that controller to tell him American 11 is not responding. But for some reason he can't quite let it go. It's playing on his mind. He switches his screen back to track American 11.

Just a precaution.

0814   **EXT BOSTON LOGAN AIRPORT**

Meanwhile, back at Boston Logan Airport, another fuel laden plane- United Airlines Flight 175 - a Boeing 767 bound for Los

Angeles - is given permission to take off.

> TOWER V/O
> This is Boston Logan Tower - United 175 you are cleared for takeoff.

Flight 175 roars down the runway and into the air.

INT. BOSTON ATC

Just like American 11 we track United 175's transponder signal in extreme close-up as it passes from Logan tower.

To Terminal Approach.

And finally into Boston Center airspace.

> CONTROLLER V/O
> United 175 you are with Boston Centre.

We pull out from the screen to find a controller accepting United 175.

As we move across to the next U area, we pass another controller asking an American flight nearby to try to contact American 11 on the company frequency.

> CONTROLLER
> American 25 – Boston Center. I need you to try and contact American 11 on company frequency. If you get him, let me know.

We move on again to yet another U area, picking up Zalewski as he continues his vigil on American 11.

It's still no show.

0818   **INT COCKPIT FLIGHT 93**

Flight 93 joins a queue of 10-15 planes awaiting take off.

> TOWER
> United 93, you're cleared on to taxiway Four Seven Bravo and hold. Takeoff runway two-two right.

                    CAPT
        Roger. United 93. Hold taxiway Four Seven Bravo.

                    TOWER
        We're expecting a 30 minute delay due to traffic.

                    CAPT
        Thanks a lot guys. You have a nice day too.

INT CABIN FLIGHT 93

Pilot Jason Dahl's voice comes over the intercom.

                    DAHL
        Morning folks. This is the captain. Looks like things are
        jammed up pretty good here at Newark this morning.
        We're anticipating about a twenty-minute delay. So sit
        back, relax. We'll let you know when we get an update
        from the tower and get you flying to San Francisco just as
        soon as we can.

It's not unusual. The skies above New York are the busiest in the world – especially at commuter hour.

In coach, Sandra Bradshaw charms the coach passengers.

In first class Burnett and Bingham, sitting across the aisle from one another, use news of the delay to break the ice. A brief interaction.

At the front Jarrah watches the line of aircraft snaking away into the distance. This is going to be a long wait.

His face says it all.

Why the delay? What does it mean?

0821   **INT BOSTON ATC**

Controller Pete Zalewski, is starting to get anxious now. Aircraft do occasionally fail to respond, but this has gone on too long.

Suddenly American 11's transponder reading disappears from his screen.

Zalewski quietly calls over his supervisor John Schippani, who gets up from his desk and walks over, leaning in from behind.

> ZALEWSKI
> I think something's wrong with American 11. The transponder signal's gone. I don't know what - it's either mechanical, electrical… but something's happened.

Schippani says he'll alert management.

We follow him as he crosses the floor back to his desk at the end of Area 'C'. He picks up the phone and begins to dial the watch desk.

Meanwhile, Zalewski switches to primary radar to track the missing aircraft.

Suddenly he hears a mysterious voice in his ear. It's heavily accented and not at all clear. Stay quiet? Returning to the airport?

Perhaps he didn't hear it right.

Then comes a second transmission. Chillingly clear.

> INTERCOM TRANSMISSION
> Nobody move, everything will be okay. If you try to make any moves, you'll endanger yourself and the airplane. Just stay quiet.

Zalewski jumps up and shouts for Schippani.

> ZALEWSKI
> John get over here immediately right now.

The other controllers in the 'U' room turn and look at him, surprised.

Schippani hurries over.

> SCHIPPANI
> Okay, calm down. What did they say? What did it sound like?

Zalewski tells him they've got a hijack. Sounded middle-eastern but he couldn't understand every word, just enough to know there's an unauthorized person in the cockpit.

We move with Schippani now, quickly out of Area C, hanging a right as he hustles down the aisle – past the mouths of other radar areas, to the Watch Desk – a square-shaped operations command area with computers and a couple of scopes comprising banks on three sides and an L-shaped ops desk in the middle.

He relays the information to the Operations Manager that American 11 has been hijacked.

Meanwhile back in Area C Zalewski is focusing. He asks Taccini to take the rest of his planes so he can concentrate on American 11 which is currently up over Albany, New York.

There are a handful of people around Zalewski's scope by now, all watching the screen, discussing the problem.

Suddenly, American 11 makes a big, unexpected turn from Northwest-bound to Southbound.

> ZALEWSKI
> Whoa! Look at that.

Something is seriously fucking wrong.

0826   **INT. FLIGHT 93**

Flight 93 crawls towards the end of the taxiway. For regular travellers on board it's a routine hazard of rush hour commuter air travel. But for the hijackers, it's a disaster.

Jarrah looks at his watch, again. He can see the World Trade Centre away in the distance.

They should be in action by now.

0828   **INT. HERNDON COMMAND CENTRE**

At the National Command Centre, Ben Sliney is at his desk running down the agenda for the morning staff meeting, when the supervisor for the East desk, Tommy Paccione approaches.

> TOMMY
> Ben, we may have a potential hijack out of Boston.

                    SLINEY
You're kidding me?!?

                    TOMMY
American flight 11, Boston – LAX

                    SLINEY
Did they get a code?

                    TOMMY
I think they may have had a hit…Boston Center thinks they heard something in the background.

                    SLINEY
Where is he now?

                    TOMMY
About 50, 60 out of Boston.

                    SLINEY
I gotta go to the 8:30. Anything develops, come in and tell me about it.

The conversation is serious, but bemused.

Sliney thinks, Jesus, the last hijacking was 10-12 years ago.

INT CONFERENCE ROOM HERNDON

The core group of Herndon managers gather in a conference room overlooking the floor.

There are two or three women, maybe four men including John White, Herndon's seasoned facilities manager and Sliney's most trusted colleague.

Sliney tells them about the suspected hijacking and they begin the routine morning call to FAA HQ with the news.

Almost immediately, Paccione comes in and whispers in Sliney's ear:

                    PACCIONE
Ben, we got more information from Boston Center. They believe a stewardess may have been stabbed on that flight.

Sliney stands up, calm but serious -

                              SLINEY
                    Excuse me. We have some information developing on the
                    hijacking.

He walks out of the meeting with Paccione in his wake, grabs a legal pad to keep notes and heads back into the operations room.

Everyone's looking at Sliney as he walks in. Some follow him to the East desk, a cluster of four consoles down at the front. Others watch from their positions. Everyone is aware there is a potential hijacking. Word of the stabbing has spread like wildfire.

Tommy asks his Boston specialists for an update while Sliney listens. They're on the phone to Boston Centre, but having a hard time getting clear information.

Sliney, frustrated, goes to his desk to call Boston Center himself.

He's told American 11 is not 'squawking' and that the plane has made a dramatic turn to the south, now heading towards New York Airspace.

Sliney instructs White to update FAA HQ of the hijacking. The duty officer there says security personnel are discussing it with the New England Regional Office. But the system is already off the rails at headquarters. The hijack coordinator is away on travel and so is his number two.

To vets like Sliney and White, it's no surprise.

They roll their eyes.

Sliney tells his staff to set up a teleconference between Boston/New York and Cleveland centers.

It's vital to keep everyone informed on this.

0834   **INT. BOSTON CENTER**

Close up on Flight 175's transponder as it moves across to the west en route to Los Angeles.

We move across to another screen, Zalewski's.

Controllers watching American 11s radar target over his shoulder, remark on the fact that the plane's speed has increased. But since the transponder is off, they don't know how high he is.

Another controller has a plane in the airspace nearby. Maybe he can see American 11 and estimate his altitude. It's United 175.

A nearby controller turns another plane to put him in a better position to see American 11. United Airlines 175

> CONTROLLER
> I'd like you to look at your twelve or one- tell me if you see an American 767.

> UA 175
> Yeah he's about 28 - 29 thousand ft.

> CONTROLLER
> Okay. Thanks. United 175 turn 30 degrees to the right. I want to keep you away from this guy.

We watch in extreme close up as United 175's transponder signal moves away to safety.

Back to American 11.

> CONTROLLER 1
> This guy's goin' fast. Look at that.

> CONTROLLER 2
> Looks like he's navigating down the Hudson.

> CONTROLLER 1
> Why the hell would he do that?

Then suddenly, another transmission.

> TRANSMISSION
> Nobody move please. We are going back to the airport. Don't try to make any stupid moves.

It hangs in the air for a beat.

> ZALEWSKI
> Someone needs to pull these fucking tapes right now!

A startled admin guy leaves.

We follow him, out of the 'U' area. Right turn, down past the watch desk.

> ADMIN GUY
> We got another transmission. He's going back to the airport. We're pulling the tapes.

He's out and on his way down to the tape room.

At the watch-desk, phones are ringing off the hook. New York Centre is reporting the same strange transmissions.

It's not protocol but the Senior Boston Manager decides to contact the military for assistance. He calls the designated Home Air Defence Centre - North Eastern Air Defence System (NEADS).

INT. NEADS HQ

A phone rings in the NEADS operations center, a large Air Force facility. Responsible for protecting the North Eastern United States.

It's a rectangular, dimly lit, high-ceilinged den. Three rows of radar consoles – about 24 in all – run the length, bifurcated down the middle by an aisle (4 on a side). Techs sit at the radar scopes, plugged in with headsets, facing a wall of 5 big screens 15' high and positioned side by side, about 80' across the wall.

In the "battle cab" that overlooks the operations floor. NEADS commander Col. Bob Marr is in the middle of his morning briefing to his battle staff.

Today's agenda, a Cold War style exercise – operation vigilant guardian - that imagines an attack by Russian bombers.

> MARR
> We have Bears penetrating the ADIZ [Air Defense Information Zone] up off Alaska. You'll want your tracker techs keeping their eyes open.

A former F-15 pilot Marr is a leader who's liked. This is his domain and the buck stops here. He still wears a flying suit.

Marr notices out of the corner of his eye that something's going on with a young sergeant down on the floor.

Tech Sgt. Jeremy Powell, 31, wandering near his console, tethered by a long headset cord, has answered the ringing phone.

> BOSTON CENTRE
> Hi. Boston centre TMU - we have a problem here. We have a hijacked aircraft headed towards New York and we need you guys to, we need someone to scramble some F-16s or something up there, help us out.

> POWELL
> Is this real-world or exercise?

> BOSTON CENTRE
> No, this is not an exercise. Not a test.

During a war game exercise, the simulations team often try to trip soldiers up. Powell, standing at his console, looks around to see if he can see the "sim" guy pretending to be Boston. Once he confirms that this is *for real* for real, he starts waving his hands.

Up in the battle cab Col. Marr sees him through the glass.

> MARR
> Go and see what that kids so excited about.

Lt. Col Dawne Deskins goes out to see what's up. Powell says he has a hijack.

> DESKINS
> A sim?

> POWELL
> No. *A no-shit hijack!*

Lt. Col. Deskins relays word of the hijacking to Marr who goes into action. But he needs his number two - Where's Nasypany?

The first of two urgent calls goes out on the PA system.

> INTERCOM
> Major Nasypany, report to the operations floor immediately.

Then another.

INTERCOM
All operations personnel report to the ops room immediately. All operations personnel report to the ops room.

Meanwhile the radios begin to buzz with overlapping conversations, updating Marr with information.

DESKINS
I'm getting reports from Boston of a possible hijack.

MARR
Any call signs?

DESKINS
It's a 757 200 series. Don't know how many people. Coming out of Boston headed for L.A.

Major Kevin Nasypany, Marrs top officer on the ops floor, is a straight shooter in his forties. As he enters the ops room and dashes onto the floor, he is immediately briefed by Marr.

MARR
We got a reported hijack out of Boston in progress. He's not squawking – find him.

As troops begin to stream in, Nasypany hustles them to take up positions.

NASYPANY
This is real world. I want people on scopes. ID people, I want you on comms. I want you on phones. I want to find out where this guy is.

TECH 1
They say he's leaving Boston Center's airspace headed towards New York.

He turns to his weapons crew. Punch up the nearest fighter base – Otis off Cape Cod – and order their two "alert" jets to battle stations. Sgt. Powell springs into action.

Marr is standing, looking out onto the floor. He confirms the order.

Otis asks the question of the hour.

OTIS
Is this real world or sim?

                         MARR
            Real world. Definitely real world.

       INT. NEWARK CONTROL TOWER

       Unaware of the trouble developing around American Flight 11,
       Tower Controller Greg Callaghan prepares Flight 93 for take-off.

                         TOWER
            United 93, runway two-two right. After departure, turn left
            to one-ninety for two-point-five, right to two-twenty.

0837   **INT. FLIGHT 93**

       As Flight 93 approaches the head of the runway, Jason Dahl
       acknowledges the tower.

                         DAHL
            Okay. Left to one-ninety for two-point-five, then right to
            two-twenty.

                         TOWER V/O
            United 93, two-two right, you are cleared for take-off.
            G'day."

0838   **EXT/INT. OTIS AIRFORCE BASE**

       Pilots grab their flight gear and prepare battle stations. Sprinting
       out to the waiting F-15s.

0840   **INT. FLIGHT 93**

       Pilot Jason Dahl instructs the cabin crew to prepare for takeoff.

       Senior stewardess, Welsh sits in the jump seat for first class. Bay
       and Green, the jump seats between first class and coach and
       Lyles and Sandy Bradshaw sit in the rear galley.

0841   **INT. NEW YORK ATC**

       A close-up of American 11's transponder as it enters New York
       Center's airspace. We hear the sound of an air traffic controller.

CONTROLLER
American 11, if you hear New York, Contact New York Center on one-two-five-point-three-two.

We pull out to reveal New York Centre controller Dave Bottiglia at his scope watching the aircraft's progress down the Hudson towards New York City.

A manager walks up and leans into Bottiglias scope.

CONTROLLER
See that target right there? Boston's logging him a hijack. American 11 out of Logan. They think he's going back to the airport. Watch him every step of the way and clear everything ahead.

Bottiglia begins clearing traffic out of American 11's way. As he works his scope, we see in extreme c/u the transponder of another airplane enter his airspace.

It's United 175.

UAL175
New York UAL 175 heavy.

BOTTIGLIA
UAL 175 go ahead.

UAL175
Yeah we figured we'd wait to go to your center. Ah, we heard a suspicious transmission on our departure out of Boston, ah, with someone, ah, it sounded like someone keyed the mikes and said ah everyone as stay in your seats.

BOTTIGLIA
Oh, okay. I'll pass that along over here.

Bottiglia returns to his main priority – tracking American 11 as it closes on New York.

Across the screen United 175's transponder quietly makes its way to the West.

Forgotten.

INT. BOSTON CENTER TAPE ROOM

The Admin guy is still trying to thread the reel-to-reel tape to play back the transmissions from American 11.

In his haste, his fingers slip and the tape tears.

"FUCK!!!"

0842 ### INT. COCKPIT. FLIGHT 93

Dahl eases the throttle back.

Flight 93's twin turbo fan Pratt & Whitney jet engines unleash 128,000lbs of thrust.

> HOMER
> Good on both engines.

More than 25 minutes late the plane finally begins to move.

> HOMER
> Groundspeed 80 knots….

100 knots.

120 knots.

0846 ### INT. CABIN. FLIGHT 93

Seasoned travelers read their books, and papers, while others grip their armrests nervously as the plane thunders down the runway.

Burnett feels the acceleration pushing him into his seat. Folds his paper and closes his eyes. At last a moment of rest.

At the rear of the plane Bradshaw checks her belt, smiles at Lyles.

We are close to full throttle now as we settle on Jarrah, eyes, closed head bowed.

Deep in prayer. Ancient Suras of war and victory.

Give us victory and may the ground shake under their feet.

Flight 93 powers up into the clear blue skies.

INT/ EXT. OTIS AIRFORCE BASE

The two F15s are ready to take off. All they need is a position, a target.

0846   **INT. NEADS HQ**

Back at NEADS Marr and Nasypany are pushing their people to find one.

                    NASYPANY
Come on, find this guy. It's a big fucking plane. American Airlines. Where's he at? What's he doing?"

One Tech calls Boston Center.

                    NEADS
This is Huntress. We need some information. We need a call sign on the possible hijack.

                    BOSTON
American 11. Last altitude we saw him at was two-nine-zero.

                    NEADS
Do you have a Mode 3?

                    BOSTON
No. We have the primary target only. We don't have any Mode 3 at all.

                    NEADS
Do you know where he's going?

                    BOSTON
No idea at all. He's headed towards Kennedy. About 40 miles out of JFK… He's having a tough time talking because they are making threats to the cockpit… The original code was fourteen-forty-three.

Meanwhile Otis Air Force Base Controllers are pushing for information.

> OTIS
> I don't know where I'm scrambling these guys to! I need a point. I need a direction. I need a destination.

> NEADS
> We've got to get a position on this guy. He was right there at the Z-point. He was heading one-nine-zero. Let's start hitting up tracks all around that Z-point.

> NEADS (TO OTIS)
> I'm gonna give you a Z-point. Just head them there.

> OTIS
> He's not squawking. He's not squawking. We can't find him.

> NEADS
> We're trying to locate this guy. What we're gonna do is light up every track from 29 thousand heading one-nine-zero.

Marr radios down to the floor.

> MARR
> Do we have radar yet?

> NASYPANY
> No, We're working on it.

NEADS controllers search their scopes in vain for American 11. But it's odd. Unfamiliar. For fifty years they've look out – across the oceans – for targets, threats. They're not used to looking inside.

Not used to it at all.

0846   **INT. FLIGHT 93**

Flight 93 rises to the northeast on a forty-five degree heading, then turns another twenty degrees to the right and follows that path four miles south towards Manhattan.

Sandra Bradshaw is still chatting with Lyles at the back of the plane.

Up front, Thomas Burnett glances out of the window as the plane banks. Then gets out a file. A balance sheet.

Jarrah stares out the window. Off to the right, the towers of the World Trade Centre pass behind the plane slowly diminishing in the distance.

Still intact.

His mind races. Has the plan failed?

A thousand thoughts.

0846 **INT. NEW YORK CENTRE**

In extreme close up we see American 11's radar return.

As we pull out we find New York Center Controller Bottiglia tracking American 11 as it bears down the Hudson Valley towards Manhattan, controllers and managers gather over his shoulder.

                    CONTROLLER 1
          Groundspeed slowing.

                    CONTROLLER 2
         He's descending…he's landing JFK?

                    CONTROLLER 1
         Or Newark?

The radar blip is right on New York.

                    CONTROLLER 1
         Got to be JFK.

And then, suddenly -

American 11 disappears from the screens.

                    BOTTIGLIA
         Where the hell did he go?

INT. NEADS HQ

On the floor, one of the ID techs gets a call. It's Boston with an update:

> NEADS
>
> Go ahead, Boston.
>
> BOSTON CENTRE
>
> Huntress, we've lost the target. I repeat, American 11, we're not seeing him. He may have descended below radar coverage. Last known position was 8 miles north of JFK.

Meanwhile in the battlecab Nasypany is telling Marr that Otis are ready to go.

Marr grabs a 'red switch'- and encrypted phone line – and punches in a code. It puts him through to General Larry Arnold at NORAD.

> MARR
> I need authority to get these guys in the air.

Arnold gives authorization and says they'll work out the permissions later.

Marr's got his scramble. He passes it to Nasypany.

Let's at least get these guys in the air.

EXT. OTIS AIRFORCE BASE

The F15s blast off into the morning sky.

0846   **INT. NEWARK CONTROL TOWER**

Controller Callahan is busy with routine traffic when the shout-line rings. Its New York ATC.

> NEW YORK TOWER
> We've lost an aircraft over Manhattan. Can you see anything out your window?

He scans the skyline.

Nothing.

Out of the corner of his eye, Callahan sees smoke rising over the Manhattan skyline.

> CALLAHAN
> Jesus! Look at that.

> ANOTHER CONTROLLER
> Looks like the World Trade Center.

> CALLAHAN
> How they gonna put that out?

0850   **INT. NEW YORK ATC**

An extreme close up of Flight 175's transponder signal traveling west.

Pull out to find Bottiglia. Now he's getting calls from other planes. One is hearing an ELT – an Emergency Locator Transponder – indicating a crashed aircraft in the vicinity.

Another calls in, asking about smoke coming off of Manhattan.

Soon there are reports that a light plane may have hit the World Trade Center.

Bottiglia turns to the controller next to him.

> BOTTIGLIA
> You've got to take my planes. I've got a hijack and a crash going on here.

In the confusion, no one notices Flight 175's transponder code suddenly change.

INT. FLIGHT 93

Flight 93 continues to climb uneventfully, blissfully unaware of the chaos behind.

Jarrah checks his watch again.

They are late. Very late.

INT. NEADS HQ

A computer maintenance tech who'd been watching CNN pokes his head into the battle cab.

> TECH
> Col. Marr, CNN's reporting a light plane hit the Trade Center. You might want to have a look.

Marr instructs one of his staffers to have them put CNN up on one of the screens on the Ops Floor. He leans close to the glass so he can see.

Down on the floor, his staff are still trying to find out what happened to American 11.

0851   **INT. NEW YORK ATC**

So is Bottiglia.

But now he notices the transponder change on United 175. It is no longer "squawking."

Bottiglia asks 175 to go back to the proper code.

> BOTTIGLIA
> United 175, contact New York Center on 23-75

No response.

He asks again. Still no response.

Following standard protocol, he makes a call to get the United to jog his transponder.

> BOTTIGLIA
> United 175 – New York Center. Recycle transponder, squawk 27-39.

No response. He calls him again.

> BOTTIGLIA
> United 175 – New York… United 175 – New York.

Bottiglia checks his radio equipment is working. It's fine. Calls to a colleague.

> BOTTIGLIA
> Anything from United 175? I'm not getting a sqwark from him?"

> COLLEAGUE
> Nothing. He's 'NORDO.'

> BOTTIGLIA
> For fuck sake as if I haven't got enough going on.

0851 **INT. FLIGHT 93**

Jarrah looks back and catches Haznawi's eye.

They both know. They are speeding away from their target with every second.

0854 **EXT. F-15 COCKPIT**

Lacking a target and unable to penetrate New York's busy civilian air traffic corridors, the F-15's are vectored toward military-controlled airspace off the Long Island coast and told to 'hold as needed'.

INT BOSTON CENTER

The admin guy, still in the Tape Room, finally mends the tape and gets the recording to play back.

Suddenly the room is filled with the voice of Mohammed Atta, leader of the 9/11 mission.

> "We have some planes. Just stay quiet and you will be okay. We are returning to the airport".

Rewind

> "We have some planes…"

Rewind

"Some planes.."

Rewind

"planes.."

Hard cut as he rushes out of the Tape Room, up the stairs, barreling, almost running, to the watch desk.

                    ADMIN GUY
          They're saying planes….some planes as in plural.

INT HERNDON COMMAND CENTER

A supervisor from the East Desk, is rushing out of his area towards Ben Sliney.

                    SUPERVISOR
          Boston Centre just pulled the tapes, the hijackers said planes.

                    SLINEY
          What the fuck does that mean?

                    SUPERVISOR
          They played back the transmissions from American 11. The hijacker said, 'We have some planes.' As in more than one plane.

A beat. As this registers.

                    SLINEY
          Are you sure about that?

                    SUPERVISOR
          Positive.

Sliney feels his adrenaline kick up a notch.

Suddenly everyone's got questions. What does that mean? How do they know? Which planes, where?

Sliney tries to inject order and process into the situation.

                    SLINEY
        Okay. First of all, we need to confirm this. Call Boston.
        See if there's anything more. Someone call headquarters,
        make sure they know about this, I don't want any
        mistakes.

                    SUPERVISOR
        You've got it.

The huddle disperses into action.

                    SLINEY
        What's the news on 11? Anything?

                    WHITE
        Nothing confirmed yet. New York's saying a light plane
        out of Ploughkeepsie just hit the Trade Centre.

                    SLINEY
        A what?

Sliney stands there, bemused. Looks up at the map with 5,000 high-altitude jets in the sky over America.

Planes!?!

0855   **INT. NEW YORK ATC**

Meanwhile, Bottiglia's calling Boston Center to see if United 175 has gone back to his original frequency. It hasn't.

                    BOTTIGLIA
        I don't like this…he must have an electrical problem or
        something. FedEx 12-72 turn 30 degrees left…

Bottiglia hands over more flights and tries to contact United 175 again.

No response.

All of a sudden, he sees United 175 make a sharp turn, and climb off course.

Bottiglia radios through to his arranger, his heart in his throat.

BOTTIGLIA
Mike get over here. I just lost United 175. I think we got another hijack.

In the same moment, a controller, Curt Applegate, who's sitting opposite Bottiglia and a few scopes down, notices the radical turn and shouts.

APPLEGATE
Hey Dave, there's an untracked target five miles east of Allentown.

Bottiglia starts turning planes out of the way of UAL 175.

BOTTIGLIA
Delta 25, I have an airplane – we don't know what he's doing. I'm going to have to turn and climb you.

He punches up the next sector he feeds to..

BOTTIGLIA
Hey, you see this target. I don't know who it is. Watch this guy. I think it's United 175, but I'm not sure.

CONTROLLER
Where's he heading?

BOTTIGLIA
Looks like New York to me.

Bottiglia, fixated on his screen, feels the fear leap a notch as United 175 starts descending ominously through heavy traffic, towards New York City.

That's when another controller two scopes to Bottiglia's right, Chris Tucker, erupts.

To his horror he realizes that United 175 is on collision course with another airliner, Delta 2315, bound for Tampa Florida. He screams into his headset.

TUCKER
Delta 2315. New York Center. Traffic 2 o'clock. 10 miles closing. I think he's been hijacked. Take any evasive action necessary. Repeat ten miles closing... 2 o'clock. Take immediate evasive action!

No one looks at Tucker – they look instead at their screens collectively holding their breath as the two blips of light converge on the screen - airplanes full of people hurtling towards each other in the sky at 500 miles-per-hour.

Bottiglia stares as they meet.

Then separate again.

The two aircraft have missed by less than 200 feet.

0857   **INT. FLIGHT 93**

In the cockpit, we hear New York Center welcome United 93.

                    CONTROLLER
      United 93, New York Center. Good morning.

Pilot Jason Dahl turns off the seatbelt sign.

Bradshaw and Lyles begin to serve a hot breakfast of omelettes and waffles to the passengers in coach.

Burnett looks up, coffee would be nice.

Jarrah watches the trolley begin its slow progress through first class.

Nothing can happen while it blocks the aisle.

0901   **INT. HERNDON COMMAND CENTER**

White takes an urgent call.

                    WHITE
      We got New York on Ben.

                    SLINEY
      Go ahead.

The call is put on speaker.

                    SLINEY
      What you got?

                              NEW YORK
          I think we've got another hijack. We have several
          situations going on here. It's escalating big, big time. We
          need to get the military involved with us. We're, involved
          with something else, we have other aircraft [meaning
          Flight 175] that may have a similar situation going on
          here.

Ben Sliney and John White exchange glances. Another hijack?!?

                              SLINEY
          Have you notified regional managers?

                              NEW YORK
          I can't get through. They're busy discussing American 11.

                              SLINEY
          Any news on that?

                              NEW YORK
          We're hearing it may have gone into the World Trade
          Centre.

                              SLINEY
          Jesus.

Behind them is the ubiquitous big screen, flickering with 5,000 airplanes.

White crosses the room. Orders up CNN on one of the large screens. Something big is happening in New York.

Now we follow White across the floor to Sliney. But Sliney's already guessed.

                              WHITE
          Ben. That's confirmed. A commercial went into the World
          Trade Centre.

                              SLINEY
          Must have been American 11.

A beat and then.

                              SLINEY
          On my first day.

INT. NEW YORK ATC

Now it's really cranking up to a pitch.

Controllers are gathering around Bottiglia watching United 175, descending fast into New York.

> APPLEGATE
> Look at him. He's dropping like a manhole cover.

It's starting to sink in: the controllers have no control. This guy is fucking reckless. Some of the controllers are getting pissed off. One slams his fist down on the console.

> CONTROLLER 2
> Those motherfuckers! This is bullshit!

Just then a manager hovering behind Bottiglia, gets a phone call.

> MANAGER 1
> They're confirming, a commercial airliner hit the World Trade Center.

> MANAGER 2
> A *commercial* airliner?!?

Suddenly, it registers.

> APPLEGATE
> This fucking guy's gonna crash.

> CONTROLLER 1
> Here comes number two. This guy's dropping 6 thousand feet a minute…

> APPLEGATE
> He's not going to Kennedy. Holy shit.

As United 175 dives, another controller calls out altitudes every 12 seconds as his radar updates.

> ANOTHER CONTROLLER
> He's doing 8 thousand feet a minute… He's at 10 thousand feet a minute… He's not going anywhere but into the ground…. He's going in. He's going straight into Midtown.

0902   **INT. NEWARK TOWER**

The 'shout phone' goes and Callahan grabs it.

> VOICE
> Where's United 175. Can you see him out your window?

Callahan scans the skyline.

He sees the incoming plane - beyond the New Jersey shipyards - flying low and fast up the Hudson river.

He grabs some binoculars and tracks it towards the Manhattan skyline.

Callaghan can't believe what he's seeing.

Its flight path is erratic banking left, then right as it streaks across the water.

Then it seems to level off slightly before starting to accelerate towards the burning WTC.

Seconds later United 175 slams into the South Tower of the WTC.

> CALLAHAN
> Oh my God! He just hit the building.

0903   **INT. HERNDON COMMAND CENTRE**

All across the floor technicians stare in horror as a giant screen captures the fireball.

Sliney's face, incredulous at what is unfolding in front of him.

INT NEADS HQ

Marr watches as his operations floor erupts in profanity and disbelief, as they watch the huge explosion on a screen.

Then a terrible silence that seems to last forever.

Incredulous technician's stare open mouthed at the flames.

Up in the battlecab Marr breaks the silence.

                        MARR
   Come on guys – get back to work. We got a job to do.

America is under attack.

0903   **INT. FLIGHT 93**

   In the cockpit pilot Jason Dahl reaches cruising altitude at 35,000 feet and puts on the autopilot.

   He chats to co-pilot Leroy Homer about sports, about overtime and other pilot stuff.

   In the cabin Senior Stewardess Deborah Welsh makes her in-flight introductions:

                        DEBORAH WELSH
   Ladies and gentlemen, shortly we will commence our in-flight entertainment service our movie today is "A Knights Tale" starring Heath Ledger – the story of 'an untrained squire who dreams of becoming a knight and assumes a false identity to compete in jousting tournaments.

   The audio for the movie can be found on Channel 1, and a Spanish version can be found on Channel 10. After this we will be playing a short-subject television comedy, followed by taped NBC news and other popular TV programming.

   We do have one request from you, that you respect the captain's judgement. As long as he does have the seat-belt sign on we request that you stay in your seat with your seat belt fastened. This is for your safety as well as the passengers' around you. At this time we ask that you sit back, relax, and enjoy your flight to San Francisco.

   Jarrah is looking intently at the cockpit door waiting to strike, looking for the perfect moment. Just then -

   Welsh introduces herself and offers him food.

0905   **INT. HERNDON COMMAND CENTRE**

Sliney is under pressure.

New York Centre calls, telling him they are declaring 'ATC Zero' no aircraft are permitted to depart from, arrive at or travel through New York's airspace until further notice.

Boston calls too, they are doing the same.

Air traffic begins to back up rapidly across the country, sending the entire National Air Traffic grid into crisis.

It's clear Sliney owns the floor now. When he speaks people listen. He's less than four hours into the job, but the shoes are beginning to fit.

Sliney goes into action, drawing on all his twenty years experience in the business.

Begins rerouting swathes of traffic from state to state. Shouting instructions – working on instinct, trying to grapple with the greatest civil aviation crisis the country has ever faced.

Meanwhile White is on a teleconference passing word of the New York and Boston ground stops to HQ in Washington.

      SLINEY
 Getting anything from them?

      WHITE
Bupkis

Sliney is being boxed in.

All he knows, all he can cling on to is that he has to protect the system, keep everything flying. That's the bottom line.

That's why he's there.

0909   **INT NEADS HQ**

Marr too, is in action.

In the battle cab and on the Ops Floor, he and his troops are "spinning up" into war footing. But it's not easy.

There are thousands of potential threats in the air, each one a civilian aircraft. But which are which?

And worse than that the planes that are friendly are simply in the way.

He needs information and airspace, and right now he's dependent on the FAA for both.

Watching the CNN coverage of the burning towers, Marr and Nasypany agree. It's time to get some military planes inside the civilian system.

> NASYPANY
> This is what I foresee that we probably need to do. We need to talk to FAA. We need to tell 'em if this stuff is going to keep on going, we need to take those fighters, put 'em over Manhattan. That's the best thing, that's the best play right now. So coordinate with the FAA. Tell them if there's more out there, which we don't know, let's get 'em over Manhattan. At least we got some kind of play.

He gives orders to tell the FAA to clear a path for the Otis fighters.

> MARR
> What other jets do we have on alert?

> STAFF
> Langley has two, sir.

> MARR
> Okay. Let's get Langley to battle stations.

> NASYPANY
> I want to get Langley up, shoot 'em over to New York and put them in the CAP.

> MARR
> No. Let's keep Langley at battle stations. Otis is gonna need some fuel in not too long, and until we can get some tankers up, Langley is our only backup. We'll swap them into the CAP when Otis hits bingo [low fuel].

Marr is being prudent. There's still so much he doesn't know.

INT/EXT. JETS

The Otis F-15s finally receive permission to enter New York airspace.

They exit their holding pattern 115 miles from New York and set a direct course for Manhattan.

0915   **INT. FLIGHT 93**

Meanwhile United 93 continues it's uneventful progress.

Most passengers are eating - some sleep, some talk. Some read. Some get ready for the movie.

There is a shudder of turbulence as they climb. A few nervous glances. Seats held tightly.

Passenger - Donald Greene is unphased. He has a pilots license - knows how to read an aircraft. Nothing to worry about.

Sandy Bradshaw is chatting with passengers Jean and Donald Peterson at the front of coach. They didn't catch the name of the film.

On the way back she tells CeeCee Lyles.

> BRADSHAW
> I'm done in ten. I'm taking my magazine. Curl up in one of those empty seats…

Up in first class Burnett is talking to Bingham – work, sports. They have a lot in common.

Mark Rothenberg eases his seat back and unfolds a newspaper.

Jarrah peers over at his three accomplices across the aisle.

Soon.

0920   **INT HERNDON COMMAND CENTRE**

The entire air traffic system is buckling now as Sliney struggles to deal with the consequences of the New York and Boston ground stops.

On top of that rumours are starting to fly. There are more planes missing. Boston are checking all inter-continental flights going west. Reports of missing or no-show aircraft are starting to flood into the Center.

Sliney directs his people to call all centers and tell them to report anything unusual immediately.

He's moving constantly around the room desperately trying to surf his way through the tidal waves of rumour and misinformation.

He instructs people from the Severe Weather section to put up a white grease board and start a tally of suspicious airplanes as reports come in from far and wide.

By now Sliney is sure it's terrorism. It has to be.

                    SLINEY
There's no way a United Airlines pilot flies into a building. No way.

White raises an eyebrow. Shakes his head.

Just then a call from Indianapolis ATC – they have been searching for American 77 for 25minutes, it deviated from its flight plan at 0854. Two minutes later its transponder disappeared. They initially assume a crash. Learning of the hijacks in New York they wonder if maybe it too has been hijacked.

                    SLINEY
Have you any idea where this aircraft is?

                  INDIANAPOLIS
Not at this time sir…. We've been searching for primary radar returns along it's course but so far nothing.

                    SLINEY
Nothing? You mean we've lost it?

                  INDIANAPOLIS
Sir……

                    SLINEY
Well keep looking – alert all centers.

He calls out for 77 to be added to the grease board.

And all the time Sliney can hear that voice in his head- "we have some planes."

But how many more? And where will they attack? And how can he keep his planes flying through this storm?

He goes over to White.

>   SLINEY
> Get on to HQ. Tell them I want to order a ground stop. We have to buy some time.

0921   **INT. COCKPIT FLIGHT 93**

Pilot Jason Dahl telexes United dispatcher Ed Ballinger a routine ACARS message from the aircraft.

>   MESSAGE
> Good mornin'..nice clb [climb] outta EWR [Newark airport] after a nice tour of the apt [apartment] courts y [and] grnd cntrl. 20 N EWC At occl [occasional] lt[ligh] chop. Wind 290/50 ain't helping. J.

INT. CABIN FLIGHT 93

Burnett looks up from his spreadsheets. Sees Al Nami across the aisle, hands fidgeting on an armrest. Al Ghamdi next to him.

Thinks nothing of it.

0923   **INT NEADS HQ**

Meanwhile in NEADS Marr is also dealing with rumour and confusion.

Unaware of the missing Flight 77, he gets confused reports that Flight 11 is still airborne and moving towards Washington.

>   BOSTON CENTER
> FAA military Boston Center. I just had a report that American 11 is still in the air and it's on its way towards – heading towards Washington.

>   NEADS
> American 11 is still in the air?

                    BOSTON CENTER
Yes.

                    NEADS
On it's way towards Washington?

                    BOSTON CENTER
It was another aircraft that hit the tower. That's the latest report we have.

                    NEADS
Okay.

                    BOSTON CENTER
I'm going to try to confirm an ID for you, but I would assume he's somewhere over either New Jersey or somewhere further south.

                    NEADS
Okay. So American 11 isn't a hijack at all, then, right?

                    BOSTON CENTER
No, he is a hijack.

                    NEADS
American 11 is a hijack?

                    BOSTON CENTER
Yes

                    NEADS
And he's going into Washington.

                    BOSTON CENTER
This could be a third aircraft.

A third aircraft? On it's way to Washington? The information shoots up the chain. Marr is stunned.

                    MARR
What the fuck is going on here? If American 11 is still flying who was the first plane into the World Trade Centre. If only the FAA could make up their minds.

Nasypany immediately scrambles the Langley fighters to the Baltimore area in order to intercept the reported Southbound American 11 on its way to Washington.

                    NASYPANY
Okay, American Airlines is still airborne – 11, the first guy.
He's heading towards Washington. Okay, I think we need
to scramble Langley right now and I'm going to take the
fighter from Otis and try to chase this guy down if I can
find him. Head them towards the Washington area… If
they're there then we'll run on them… These guys are
smart.

EXT. LANGLEY AIRFORCE BASE AIRSTRIP

The Langley F15 pilots Captain Honey and Major Lou prepare for take off.

0924   **INT/EXT. JET. SKY OVER MANHATTAN**

Meanwhile the two Otis F-15s reach Manhattan and establish a Combat Air Patrol.

From the lead cockpit the pilot can see the World Trade Centre Towers ablaze in the distance.

0924   **INT. CLEVELAND ATC**

Close up on Flight 93s transponder as it arrives into Cleveland airspace. America's busiest air traffic crossroads. We pull out to meet the Cleveland controller as he accepts the aircraft.

                    CLEVELAND CONTROLLER
Flight 93. This is Cleveland centre on seven two five zero.

0924   **INT. COCKPIT FLIGHT 93**

Flight 93 replies.

                    DAHL
Morning Cleveland, United Ninety-three with you at, three-five-oh (35,000 feet), intermittent light chop.

                    CLEVELAND
United ninety-three, Cleveland, roger.

Leroy Homer sees an ACARS message flash up on the screen for him.

                    MESSAGE
        Your wife wants to know if you're okay.

Tears the message off. That's odd. She's never sent a message before.

A few minutes later another message flashes up. Dahl prints it out. It's from United dispatcher, Ed Ballinger.

                    MESSAGE
        Beware any cockpit intrusion –
        Two A/C hit World Trade Center.

Dahl shows the message to Homer.

                    DAHL
        What the hell does that mean?

                    HOMER
        Something obviously going on in New York.

Dahl punches in a reply.

                    MESSAGE
        Ed confirm lastest message plz– Jason.

0925   **INT OPERATIONS CENTRE HERNDON**

Silence up above. Chaos down below.

Sliney's in the middle of it. Waiting for that phone to ring. For a decision to be made. For something to be done.

He buttonholes the Air Force "bird" colonel based in Herndon and asks him if he knows anything.

He doesn't and retreats to his cipher-locked office, to seek advice.

On the white board the numbers of suspect aircraft are mounting.

Boston ATC are calling. After reviewing all trans-continental departures out of Boston Logan they too have a missing plane - a possible hijack - Delta 89.

Meanwhile American 77 is still missing heading who knows where? Sliney looks at the map. Could it be Chicago? The Sears Tower perhaps?

Sliney walks over to White, who's on the phone with FAA.

SLINEY
Anything?

White just rolls his eyes.

Sliney looks at the screens filled with thousands of tiny dots. At the room full of people looking to him, their frustration peaking. He's got to do something.

SLINEY
No one else takes off. I want a groundstop immediately.

WHITE
You got it.

At least they've bought some time.

0927 **INT. FLIGHT 93**

The toilet near the cockpit is engaged.

Haznawi gets up, hovers by the door clutching a wash bag.

Jarrah watches intently.

The vacant light flashes on and a passenger exits.

Al Nami and Al Ghamdi watch Haznawi go into the toilet.

INT. TOILET FIRST CLASS CABIN

Haznawi begins to unpack from a washbag the pieces that we saw earlier. He unravels the wire and connects it to the battery. Winds red tape around it. Then the children's clay. Buries two clips and connects them to the battery.

He tightens the 'bomb' around his waist with a black belt.

INT. FIRST CLASS CABIN

Jarrah is staring at the 'engaged' light intently.

So is Al Ghamdi. So is Al Nami

The light flicks to 'vacant.'

Haznawi opens the door and exits, the bomb concealed by his jacket.

One last glance at Jarrah, then Al Nami and Al Ghamdi. He takes his seat.

Ready.

INT. COACH /FIRST CLASS CABIN

We follow Deborah Welsh now, as she walks back to the first class galley next to the cockpit door.

Al Ghamdi rises and heads towards the toilet.

Closer.

Closer.

He grabs Welsh, holding a knife to her throat. Turns her and displays her to the cabin.

     AL GHAMDI
 Allahu Akbar!

For a moment the first class passengers are stunned, not quite understanding.

Mark Rothenberg gets to his feet.

     MICKEY ROTHENBERG
 Hey listen. Whatever you want there's…

In one swift movement Haznawi, seated behind him, pulls his head back and stabs him savagely in the neck.

Now everyone will understand.

Passengers scream.

Now Al Nami stands too shouting and spraying pepper spray into peoples faces brandishing a knife.

More screams.

Haznawi now opens his jacket, brandishing the "bomb" and screaming at the terrified passengers.

Together they herd the passengers back into coach.

Through all this, Jarrah sits quietly…

INT. GALLEY/ COCKPIT.

Now Jarrah springs to his feet.

Welsh is still being held at knifepoint by Al Ghamdi.

> JARRAH
> Open the door and no one will get hurt. I want to see the pilot. Do it, or you will die.

The knife is at her throat.

Trained to co-operate in hijack situations Welsh knocks on the cockpit door for access.

Three and one.

INT. COACH/ REAR OF THE PLANE.

In coach people are standing up, wondering what's going on. Trying to find out what the commotion is. Bradshaw is still serving breakfast.

The curtain whips open as terrified first class passengers pour in.

They've got a bomb, they've got a bomb.

Panic spreads through the cabin like wildfire.

At the back of the plane Bradshaw stows the trolley and asks what is going on?

Meanwhile Haznawi and Al Nami are forcing the choking passengers down the plane.

>   HAZNAWI
>   Get back. Get back!

Rothenberg falls to the floor in the aisle bleeding heavily. Gronlund calls for anyone to help.

Several passengers grab him and they stagger to the rear cabin.

Eventually people find seats and gaze in shock at the scene of horror unfolding in front of them.

Then the hijackers draw the curtain between coach and first class.

Now they're blind.

0928 **INT. FLIGHT 93 COCKPIT**

Homer opens the cockpit door carrying his breakfast tray.

With one arm around Welsh's neck, using her body as a shield, Al Ghamdi stabs him.

From his seat, Dahl sees only a mass of bodies. Shouting, grunting, groaning.

INT. CLEVELAND AIR TRAFFIC CONTROL

A Cleveland Controller receives a sudden radio transmission from Flight 93.

Violent. Abstract. Frightening.

The controller responds, "Somebody call Cleveland?"

INT. FLIGHT 93 COCKPIT

Now Homer falls to the floor.

Al Ghamdi steps into the cockpit.

Plunges his knife into Dahl's chest and neck.

In the struggle Dahl knocks the column and keys the radio a second time.

INT CLEVELAND AIR TRAFFIC CONTROL

The controller hears the sound of screaming. Fighting. And a voice

>   TRANSMISSION
> Hey get out of here – get out of here – get out of here.

The controller knows what's been happening in New York. Knows immediately what this is.

It's another hijack.

0929   **INT. COCKPIT FLIGHT 93**

Jarrah takes the co-pilots seat and grabs the controls. He immediately tries to correct the steep decent that has occurred during the struggle.

The hijackers pull Dahl out from his jump seat. Drag his body out of the cockpit and dump it next to Homer's by the first class galley.

INT. CABIN FLIGHT 93

Passengers panic as the plane starts to pitch erratically. What's going on? What's happening?

Bradshaw and the other stewardesses order people to strap into their seats and stay quiet.

She is still trying to work out what just happened.

INT. COCKPIT FLIGHT 93

Jarrah is frantically trying to disengage the autopilot. Multiple alarms are triggered.

>   ALARM
> Sink rate. Sink rate. Pull up. Pull up.

0930   **INT. CLEVELAND ATC**

The controller watches Flight 93's sharp decent and tries to raise the pilot with no success.

> CONTROLLER
> United 93. This is Cleveland Centre
> United 93 please respond. This is Cleveland Centre.

He begins a desperate operation to move other aircraft out of Flight 93's path.

0930   **EXT. LANGLEY HQ**

The two Langley F15s take off heading for Baltimore to intercept American 11, which they believe is en route to Washington.

They know nothing about Flight 93.

INT. NEADS

As the F15s streak towards an encounter with the phantom American 11, Nasypany raises a crucial question with Marr.

> NASYPANY
> We have hijacked planes. What are we going to do? Langley is scrambled. I'm gonna have to tell my guys, what do they do when they get there? What is it - nine's in the nose?

Marr tells him he's just been on with General Arnold. They're talking about shooting down a commercial airliner.

Nasypany looks up at him.

They're crossing a threshold.

0932   **INT. FLIGHT 93**

In the cockpit Jarrah is still struggling with the controls.

It's the first time he's ever actually flown a plane. It's not easy. Height and speed vary frantically. Alarms sound as he tries to override the autopilot.

He holds down the microphone, apparently unaware he is heard by Cleveland Center.

> JARRAH
> Ladies and Gentlemen: Here the captain, please sit down keep remaining sitting. We have a bomb on board. So, sit.

Meanwhile Al Ghamdi watches Welsh as she tends the stricken pilots.

0932 **INT. CLEVELAND CENTRE**

The Cleveland controller receives Jarrah's message and pretending not to hear, responds:

> CLEVELAND CONTROLLER
> Calling Cleveland Centre. You are unreadable. Say again, slowly.

As he frantically moves planes out of the way of United 93 he shouts out to his supervisor.

> CLEVELAND CONTROLLER
> We got another one. United 93…

The supervisor barrels down the aisle to the Management Desk to break the news.

Meanwhile other planes are calling in.

They too have heard the sounds of struggle and death in flight 93's cockpit.

0932 **INT. FLIGHT 93**

At the back of the plane passengers huddle in groups.

They can see the two hijackers, Al Haznami and Al Nami watching them from a distance.

Occasionally, the hijackers shout warnings and wave what looks like a bomb. But they don't get too close.

Amidst the terror passengers try to work out what happened.

Burnett in first class was one of the few witnesses. But it was all so quick.

Were those knives?

Did they have a gun? There was a bomb too, right? It can't be. How could they get it on the plane? How could this happen? To them? Out in the clear blue sky?

How many hijackers were there? Three? No Four. No three. Are they Cuban? If they're Cuban they'll want to land and negotiate.

No, they were Middle Eastern. Someone remembers there were Arab men in first class - but they're not sure how many.

Burnett tries to inject order and process into the situation. Bingham breaks in occasionally. Everyone wants to help.

We have to gather information.

Meanwhile at the back Wanda Green is telling what she saw to Sandra Bradshaw and the other stewardesses. They also are trying to work out what just happened.

It's a hijacking. The plane will land. A deal, will be struck. Then they will be released. We just have to stay calm. Remember our training – co-operate. Don't draw attention to yourself.

Bradshaw tries to call the cockpit.

No answer.

She replaces the receiver. Looks at her shaking hands. Why me? Why this flight. I want to see my family again.

0932   **INT. HERNDON COMMAND CENTRE. DAY**

Suddenly White yells at Sliney.

WHITE
We got something.

SLINEY
What?

                              WHITE
                Dulles have got an unidentified aircraft tracking eastward
                at high speed…into Washington.

"No…Not another one " thinks Sliney.

0936   **INT. COCKPIT FLIGHT 93**

            Al Ghamdi brings Welsh back into the cockpit.

            She begins to plead for her life as a new ACARS message flashes
            across the screen. It's a "High Security Alert."

            Just do it. Do it, Jarrah tells Al Ghamdi as he wrestles with the
            controls.

            Struggling to the last, Welsh is killed. A horrendous scene.

            As a new message comes in from United dispatch:

            "Can dispatch be of any assistance?"

0934   **INT NEADS HQ**

            Up in the battlecab, Marr is organizing logistics, as the Towers
            burn on the giant screens in front of him.

                              MARR
                    Generate. Generate. Generate.
                    I want planes, tankers, C130s, Tomahawks.
                    Whatever they've got, I want them….

            NEADS controllers cajole, threaten, bribe – anything to get
            mobilized.

                              NEADS CONTROLLER
                    If I could shit an F16 right now I would.

            A gigantic military machine is stirring to life.

0936   **INT FLIGHT 93**

            Sandra Bradshaw sits in the first seat at the back of coach.

She makes a call to United Airlines. At first she's held in an automated queue.

Shit!!

Finally she reaches an operator and tells her that the plane has been hijacked. The hijackers are in the cabin behind the first-class curtain and in the cockpit. They've announced that they have a bomb. They've killed a flight attendant.

She tries to keep calm, professional, act according to training. But it's hard to re-assure anyone when the group of passengers up front tending Mickey Rothenberg say they can't feel a pulse and he's dead.

Tom Burnett also calls. Tells his wife the news. A passenger has been stabbed. Call 911.

Meanwhile, Mark Bingham makes a furtive, hurried call to his mother. Tells her his flight has been hijacked.

              MARK BINGHAM
    Three guys and they say they have a bomb. You believe
    me don't you mum?

Sandra Bradshaw moves forward to check on the injured passenger. It's clear he's dead.

Whilst there she looks up towards the front of the plane. At that moment the curtain moves as a hijacker goes back to the cockpit.

She catches a glimpse of two bodies lying on the floor outside the cockpit. Clearly the pilot and co-pilot. She goes into the galley to fetch some water. We see her struggling for composure.

Tom Burnett can see that she has seen something. But what?

Soon word spreads around the plane. Just from the reaction of the stewardesses, observant passengers can tell. This is no ordinary hijack.

The pilots are dead. The hijackers are actually flying the plane.

0936   **INT. HERNDON COMMAND CENTRE**

Sliney gets word that the unidentified aircraft closing on

Washington is minutes away. A C-130 is tracking him.

Sliney thinks for fuck's sake – where are the military. When is someone going to do something?

This isn't supposed to happen.

Then Cleveland Center are patched in. United Flight 93 from Newark to San Francisco is presumed hijacked. A suspected bomb on board.

Controllers are tracking its progress and moving planes out of its path.

Jesus Christ, thinks Sliney, looking at the white board – that's four.

0936   **INT. NEADS HQ**

A call comes in from Boston Centre.

A tech runs across the floor towards Nasypany.

> TECH
> Sir. Reports of an unidentified aircraft closing on Washington.

Nasypany moves to an ID site and hears Boston Centre reporting in.

> BOSTON CENTRE
> Latest report, aircraft VFR (visual flight rules) 6 miles southwest of the White House – six southwest of the White House – deviating away.

Marr is stunned.

Is this a third plane, or did they miss American 11? He authorizes Nasypany to take immediate control of FAA airspace and clear a path for the two Langley fighters.

> NASYPANY
> Okay, we're going to turn it up… crank it up… Run them to the White House."

But to his horror he discovers that, the fighters are not headed north towards Baltimore as he instructed, but east over the ocean.

                    NASYPANY
    Where are my Langley guys? Where are my Langley
    guys?

The weapons tech gives coordinates – 60 miles out over the Atlantic.

                    NASYPANY
    What the fuck are they doing out there?!? I don't care
    how many windows you break, damn it! Okay, Push them
    back!

Marr thunders in. It's getting tense on the floor.

                    MARR
    What's going on. Why are you turning
    planes around?"

                    NASYPANY
    I'm getting bad shit from the FAA.

EXT. JETS OVER WATER.

The Langley fighters turn and streak back towards Washington.

0936

EXT .WASHINGTON DAY

The Capitol Building.

People jogging, tourists taking photos of monuments.

Defenceless.

INT. WASHINGTON REAGAN AIRPORT TOWER.

Chris Stephenson, controller-in-chief at Reagan Tower is on the "shout-phone" speaking with the Secret Service giving them an update on the inbound aircraft.

                    STEPHENSON
    Five miles out from the White House.

Stephenson can see it on the radar now closing.

                              STEPHENSON
                    Four miles from the White House.

Chris Stephenson checks the skyline as news comes in that the
Secret Service are evacuating the White House

                              STEPHENSON
                    Yeah I've got a visual.

He picks out American 77 flying fast and low.

It banks and circles with chilling precision.

Picking its moment.

Then it disappears behind a building in nearby Crystal City and
explodes sending a fireball 200ft into the air.

INT. NEADS

A desperate scramble.

Marr wants updates on the fighters. How far are they from
Washington? What's their ETA?

Where is the target?

But it's too late.

0938   **INT. LANGLEY FIGHTERS**

The Langley fighters finally arrive over Washington. The pilots
see smoke rising from the Pentagon as they circle the capital.

                              PILOT
                    Looks like that aircraft crashed into the Pentagon, Sir.

INT. NEADS

The Pentagon.

Nasypany looks at Marr.

Marr takes this in. You can feel what it means throughout the room.

From now on whether it's official or not Marr believes he is at war.

He tells Nasypany - the FAA has no choice now. They have to get out of the way.

0939   **INT. FLIGHT 93**

Jarrah makes another cockpit announcement.

>   JARRAH
> Uh, is the captain. Would like you all to remain seated. There is a bomb on board and are going back to the airport, and to have our demands. Please remain quiet.

He looks across at Al Nami praying in the cockpit next to him.

Pulls' the control column to the left.

0939   **INT CLEVELAND CENTRE**

The Cleveland controller responds to Jarrah.

>   CLEVELAND CENTRE
> United 93, understand you have a bomb onboard. Go ahead.

There is no reply.

He sees the plane start to turn.

Where the hell is he going?

0940   **INT FLIGHT 93**

Burnett looks out of the window. So does Sandy Bradshaw. The plane is definitely making a turn.

They look for landmarks, contours, anything that might enable them to find their bearings.

                              GREENE
            It's turning south-east.

How do you know? Asks a fellow passenger.

                              GREENE
            I'm a pilot.

Meanwhile Thomas Burnett calls his wife for a second time and tells her that the hijackers are in the cockpit. The man who was knifed is dead. He tried to help but felt no pulse.

He is told two planes have hit the World Trade Centre. He relays this information to Mark Bingham and other passengers nearby.

Then he returns to the phone and fires new questions - were they definitely commercial planes? Which airlines? How many?

Panic fights a war with control as it starts to dawn on them that this too might be a suicide mission.

Glick calls his wife to check the details. She reports the same grim facts.

The stewardesses are still telling people to stay calm.

That's not going to work, says Burnett.

Not now.

Sandy Bradshaw looks at him. Knows it's true.

0941   **INT CLEVELAND CENTRE**

            The controller tracks Flight 93 south east towards Washington.

            INT NEADS HQ

            Marr starts launching jets, but with no clear rules of engagement. There are near-misses between military aircraft and airliners as the jets blast off.

            But Marr is focused only on bringing the military into the field. They have to impose themselves on the situation.

            He still knows nothing about Flight 93.

0942   **INT HERNDON COMMAND CENTRE**

Sliney is under pressure as never before.

News of the Pentagon strike is flooding in. It's up there live on the big screens.

The military is stirring into war-mode. They want civilian planes out of their way. Air Force One is now airborne and holding at high altitude. The Vice President has been evacuated from the White House. Military planes are taking off into civilian airspace.

There's a report of a near miss in the South as fighters blast off to protect Air Force One but come dangerously close to a commercial plane.

The military want to own the skies. Sliney can feel it.

United 93 is closing on Washington. Delta 89 is still possibly heading towards Chicago.

There are almost a dozen other suspect aircraft.

But even the groundstop is not enough.

White walks over.
                              WHITE
            It's not working Ben. We can't keep flying through this…

Sliney knows it.

Walks away on his own for a moment.

White knows what he's thinking.

It's not meant to be like this. Strikes, bad weather, system failures - they can all be managed.

But this? This is unique. And it's beaten them.

He walks back to White.
                              SLINEY
            I'm thinking of shutting down the system.

White puts his hand on Sliney's shoulder. Knows the

consequences for Sliney's career if he's wrong. For the first time all day he asks:

> WHITE
> You sure you want to do that, Ben?

> SLINEY
> It's our only choice.

A beat.

> SLINEY
> I'm doing it.

The order goes out. Clear the skies.

0944 **INT FLIGHT 93**

Burnett leans down beneath the seat and calls his wife for the third time.

He learns that a third plane just hit the Pentagon.

He tells her that a group of passengers are talking about doing something. He doesn't think the bomb is real.

Deena insists he stay quiet, and not draw attention to himself, but Burnett is now determined.

We have to do something, he says, and rings off.

0949 **INT HERNDON COMMAND CENTRE**

Flight 93 is getting closer.

The specialist on the phone with Cleveland is getting increasingly agitated with each update. He passes them to White who's on the phone with FAA HQ.

Then conflicting reports. Sliney is informed that they have lost track of United 93 over the Pittsburg area.

> SLINEY
> You've lost it?

Then the Secret Service calls and says United 93 has hit Camp David.

What that can't be right thinks Sliney. Then another call from Indianapolis.

> CONTROLLER
> Twenty-nine minutes out of Washington DC.
> ETA 10.15

United 93 is still flying.

Someone at HQ has to request military assistance.

> FAA HQ
> They're pulling Jeff away to talk about Flight 93.

> WHITE
> Uh, do we want to think, uh, about scrambling aircraft?

> FAA HQ
> Oh, God, I don't know.

> WHITE
> Uh, that's a decision somebody's gonna have to make probably in the next ten minutes.

> FAA HQ
> Uh, ya know everyone just left the room.

Sliney can barely contain his frustration.

Why aren't they making decisions?

And still Flight 93 is closing on Washington.

0949   **INT FLIGHT 93**

Amidst the terror and panic, a debate rages on the plane.

What are we going to do?

If we do nothing we're gonna die. We have to do something. Burnett, Bingham, Beamer and Glick are all up for trying. They know there's a passenger, Donald Greene, who says he could fly the plane.

The time for "Sit down, be quiet and don't draw attention to yourself." Is long gone.

The time for pre-emptive strike has come.

We have to get them before they get us.

Burnett goes to the back of the plane. Bingham and Glick follow.

They tell Bradshaw and the other stewardesses that they're forming a plan.

> BURNETT
> Are you prepared for a counter-attack?

They ask Bradshaw if she knows the plane. The strength of the cockpit door. It's weakest point.

They allocate various roles to each other. Sandra Bradshaw offers to boil hot water to throw in the hijackers faces. Wanda Green goes to the fridge and takes out a bottle of wine, wraps it in a towel and smashes its base.

They look around for any other weapons - metal cutlery, crockery, a fire extinguisher.

The fight back will be messy, brutal, improvised.

On the way back the rest of the passengers aware of what's being planned make their views known. A vote of sorts is taken.

Passengers begin to call loved ones, hoping and praying that it's not for the last time.

Marion Britton calls her friend Fred, tells him about the hijack. She knows about the World Trade Centre.

She then passes the phone to the passenger next to her.

Honor Elizabeth Wainio, takes the phone and dials her stepmother.

> WAINIO
> Mom, we're being hijacked. I just called to say good-bye.

In another area Linda Gronlund is calling her sister.

                    GRONLUND
          Hi, Else, this is Lin. I just wanted to tell you how much I
          love you. Please tell Mom and Dad how much I love them.
          I don't know if I'm ever going to get a chance to tell you
          again in person how much I love you, but I'm really going
          to miss you.

Next to her, boyfriend Joe DeLuca has just called his father.

Back at his seat now, Tom Burnett also calls his wife for the last time. For the first time there is emotion in his voice.

                    BURNETT
          Pray, just pray, Deena.

INT HERNDON COMMAND CENTRE

A visual report from another aircraft, Flight 93 is now 20 miles northwest of Johnstown, closing on Washington fast.

Sliney is angry now.

They're running out of time.

0955   **INT FLIGHT 93 COCKPIT**

Jarrah punches a new code into the automatic pilot system. It's the waypoint for Reagan National airport.

Takes out a visual aid from amongst some papers and puts it on the clipboard.

A postcard showing an aerial view of the Capitol Building.

EXT. WASHINGTON DAY

The Capitol building is being evacuated.

Police cars. People hurrying down steps. Loud hailers.

Panic and confusion in the capital.

0957   **INT FLIGHT 93**

The passengers are waiting until they're over a remote rural area.

Flight attendant Sandy Bradshaw calls her husband. She tells him the flight she's on has been hijacked. She will give up flying is she survives this.

> BRADSHAW
> We're all back here getting hot water together and getting ready to take over the plane.

Beamer is at an airphone reciting the Lord's Prayer with Verizon operator Lisa Jefferson.

Bingham and Burnett join in nearby.

> BEAMER
> For mine is the Kingdom, and the power, and the glory, forever and ever. Amen.

CeeCee Lyles, calls her husband.

> LYLES
> They're getting ready to force their way into the cockpit.

It is a strange atmosphere. Stoicism, praying, weeping - all the passengers now know the moment is upon them.

Meanwhile up in the cockpit, the hijackers are praying to their God.

Al Ghamdi bursts in and tells them that something is being planned at the back of the plane.

Heated exchanges in Arabic.

With Al Ghamdi in the cockpit, the passengers see the chance they need.

A voice says "Are you guys ready? Let's roll."

The passengers, Burnett and Bradshaw amongst them, rush at Haznawi.

A desperate struggle.

The hijacker is killed and they discover the bomb is fake.

Adrenalin and exhilaration spread like wildfire around the back of the plane.

The pre - emptive strike is working.

Meanwhile Al Ghamdi has come back down the cabin and sees that the passenger revolt has begun.

He runs back towards the cockpit.

Empowered by their first small victory others step up too, fear and adrenalin making it impossible to stay seated.

The passengers charge on towards the cockpit.

A desperate last fight begins.

0958   **INT. COCKPIT**

Jarrah disengages the autopilot and begins to rock the plane violently from side to side, in an attempt to throw the passengers off balance, as they make their way up to the cockpit.

Still the assault continues.

Jarrah changes tactic and pitches the nose of the plane up and down in order to disrupt the assault.

There are loud thumps crashes, shouts and breaking glass and plates, as passengers are hurled around the cabin.

Still the attack continues.

Now some have reached the galley outside the cockpit door.

Jarrah pitches the nose of the aircraft up and down.

For everyone on board, this has become the flight from hell.

But still the assault continues.

Several passengers try to manhandle a galley trolley into position.

In the cockpit Jarrah stabilizes the plane. Five seconds later he asks –

> JARRAH
> Is that it? Shall we finish it off?" A hijacker responds, "No. Not yet. When they all come, we finish it off.

A passenger shouts, "In the cockpit. If we don't, we'll die!"

Sixteen seconds later, another shouts, "Roll it!"

The sound of violent impacts as the dining trolley smashes into the door.

Still the passengers attack.

A hijacker shouts, "Allah is the greatest! Allah is the greatest!" He then asks, "Is that it? I mean, shall we put it down?"

The passengers are almost in the cockpit now.

A hijacker shouts, yes "Put it in it and pull it down!"

The passengers are seconds away from overpowering them.

A hijacker says, "Pull it down. Pull it down."

The airplane heads down; the control wheel turned hard to the right.

A hijacker shouts, "Allah is the greatest. Allah is the greatest."

By now the cockpit voice recording has become an indistinct shriek of wind noise.

The cockpit door opens. Hands grasp desperately for the control column.

Other hands resist as the plane rolls on it's back.

Hijackers and passengers struggle for control of the plane.

It turns nose down and ploughs into an empty field at 580 miles per hour.

HARD CUT TO BLACK.

EXT. SHANKSVILLE. PENNSYLVANIA. DAY

Fade up - an aerial shot of smoke billowing from the ground. Slowly we begin to hear:

> WASHINGTON CENTER
> We have reports of another hijack – United 93 out of Newark – we're getting reports they have a bomb on board.

> NEADS
> A bomb on board? It's United 93?

> ANOTHER TECH (in background)
> A bomb!

> FAA
> Correct. United 93. Consider him a hijack.

EXT. SHANKSVILLE. PENNSYLVANIA. DAY

Fade up another view of the smoking ground.

> NEADS
> I also want to give you a heads-up, Washington.

> FAA
> Go ahead.

> NEADS
> United nine three, have you got information on that yet?

> FAA
> Yeah, he's down.

> NEADS
> He's down?

> FAA
> Yes.

NEADS
When did he land? 'Cause we have got confirmation.

FAA
He did not land.

NEADS
Oh, he's down? Down?

FAA
Yes. Somewhere up northeast of Camp David.

NEADS
Northeast of Camp David.

EXT. WASHINGTON. DAY

We begin to hear a montage of different Air Traffic Control frequencies – pilots requesting guidance, clarification, exemption - as all over America civilian planes are forced to land.

The montage builds and builds and builds until finally a single military voice.

VOICE
The Vice President has cleared us to intercept tracks of interest and shoot them down if they do not respond.

We will take lives in the air to save lives on the ground.

EXT. MANHATTAN ISLAND. DAY

Fade up smoke billowing into the sky over Manhattan.

Suddenly, dark fighter jets streak across the sky - powerful, unfamiliar, ominous.

STILLS

Cheyenne Jackson as passenger Mark Bingham.

Jonathan Olley

Trish Gates, as flight attendant Sandra Bradshaw, conducts a routine passenger check on United Airlines Flight 93.

Omar Berdouni, as hijacker Ahmed Al Haznawi, prepares to board.

National Operations Manager Ben Sliney at the Command Center in Herndon, Virginia, as himself.

Lewis Alsamari *(left)* as hijacker Saeed Al Ghamdi and Jamie Harding as hijacker Ahmed Al Nami.

Actors portraying air traffic controllers at the Newark Airport Control Tower witness the attack beginning to unfold on September 11th.

(left to right) Daniel Sauli as Richard Guadagno, David Alan Basche as Todd Beamer, and Denny Dillon as Colleen Fraser.

Actors portraying passengers of United Airlines Flight 93 prepare their retaliation plan.

FAA operations manager Ben Sliney (on the phone) as himself, surrounded by air traffic controllers.

Actors portraying passengers on United Airlines Flight 93.

(left to right) Starla Benford and Trish Gates as flight attendants Wanda Green and Sandra Bradshaw.

Becky London and Tom O'Rourke as Jean and Donald Peterson.

Patrick St. Esprit as NEADS mission crew commander Kevin Nasypany.

(left to right) Trish Gates as Sandra Bradshaw, Tara Hugo as Kristin White Gould, Erich Redman as Christian Adams, and Opal Alladin as CeeCee Lyles.

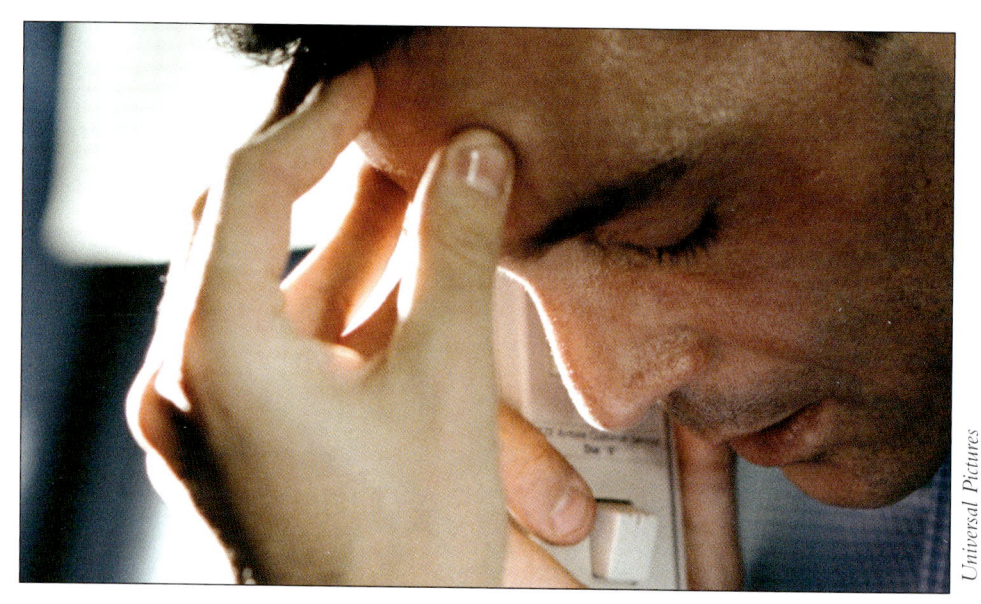

David Alan Basche, as passenger Todd Beamer, tries to reach home.

Actors portraying passengers of United Airlines Flight 93 prepare to fight back against their hijackers.

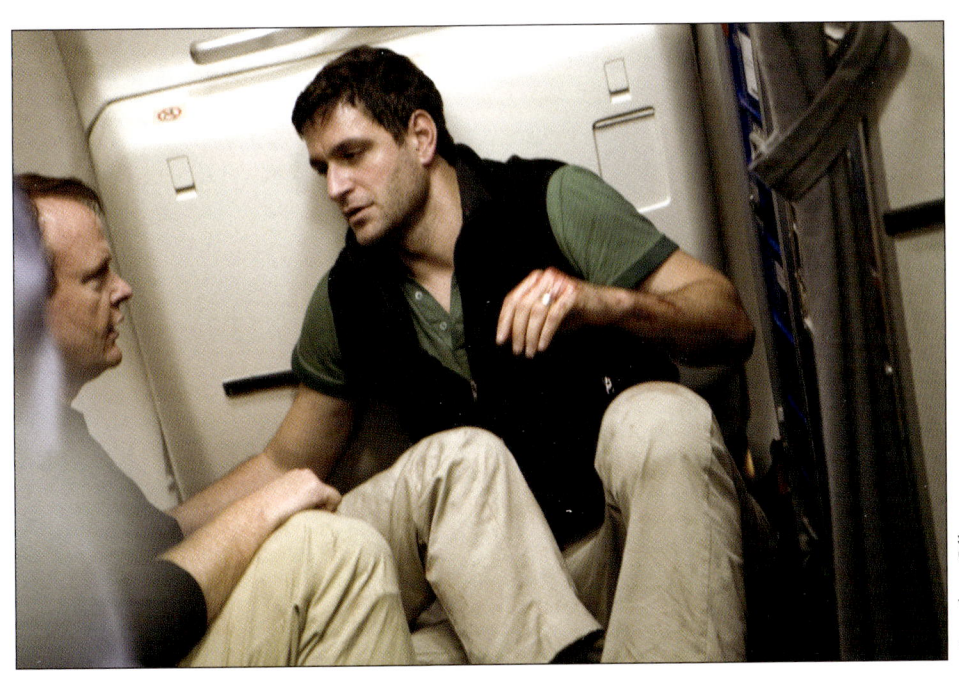

Christian Clemenson as Thomas E. Burnett, Jr., and Peter Hermann as Jeremy Glick.

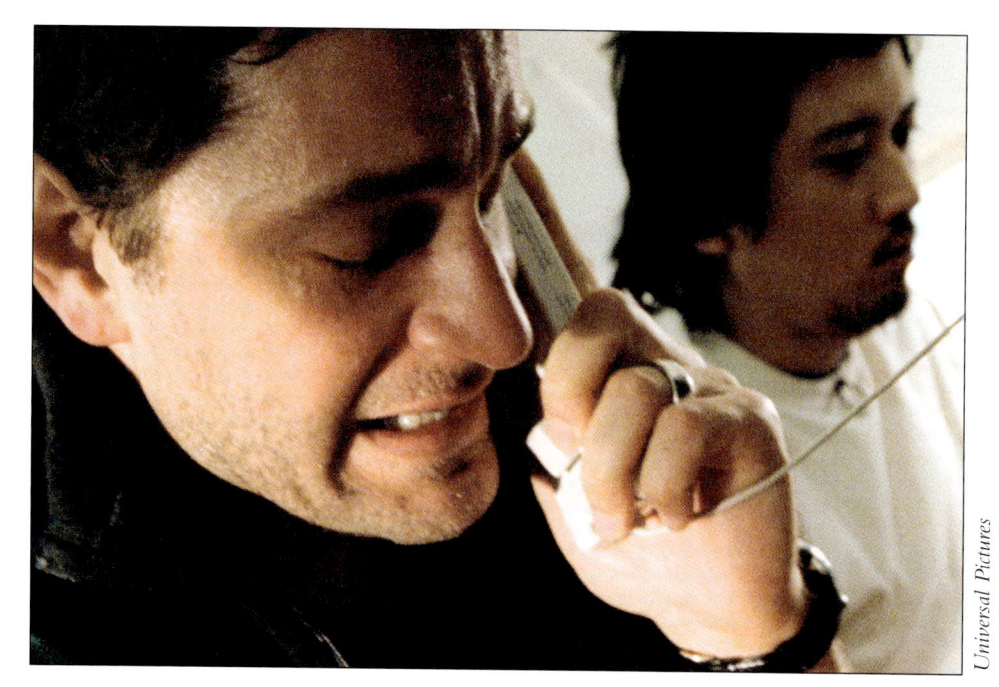

(left to right) Peter Hermann as Jeremy Glick and Masato Kamo as Toshiya Kuge.

(left to right) Rebecca Schull as Patricia Cushing and Susan Blommaert as Jane Folger grapple with their plight.

(left to right) Corey Johnson as Louis J. Nacke, II, David Alan Basche as Todd Beamer, Christian Clemenson as Thomas E. Burnett, Jr., and Cheyenne Jackson as Mark Bingham.

Christian Clemenson as Thomas E. Burnett, Jr.

Actors portraying crew and passengers of United Airlines Flight 93 charge to reclaim the plane from the hijackers.

Writer/director/producer Paul Greengrass with the actors who portray the crew and passengers of United Airlines Flight 93.

Writer/director/producer Paul Greengrass with cast members on the set.

Writer/director/producer Paul Greengrass with the actors who portray the hijackers.

SHOTS FROM BEHIND THE SCENES

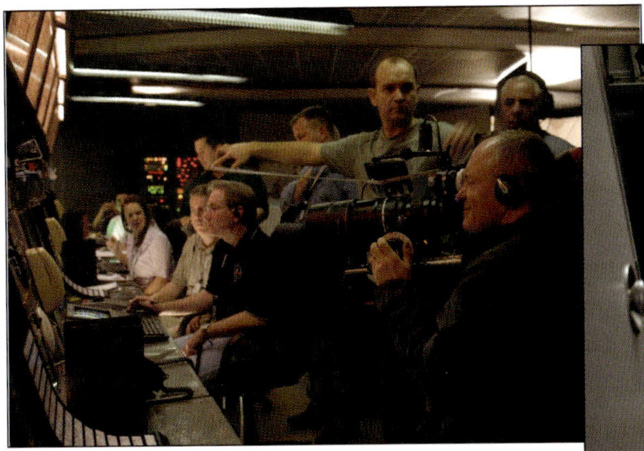

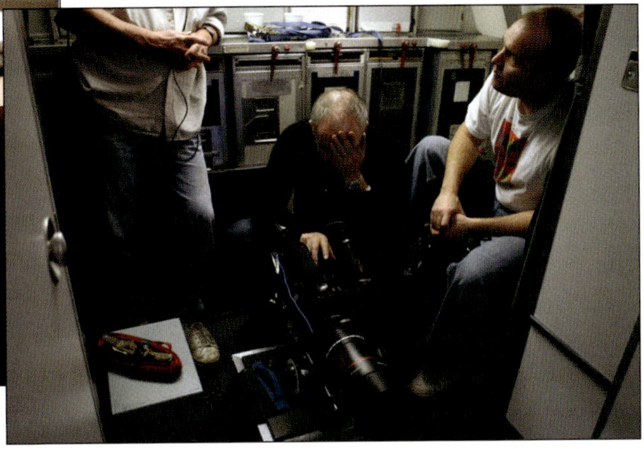

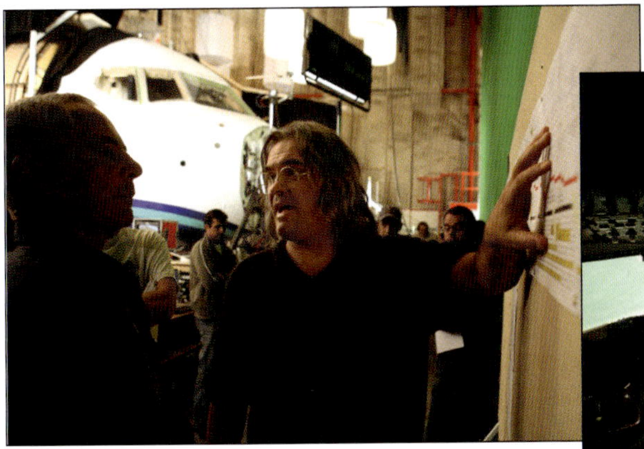

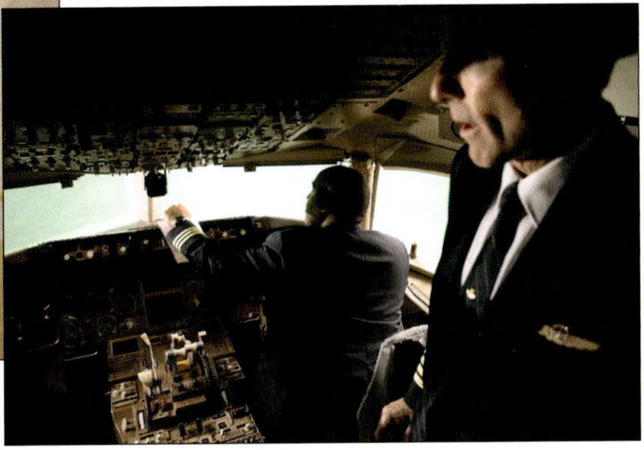

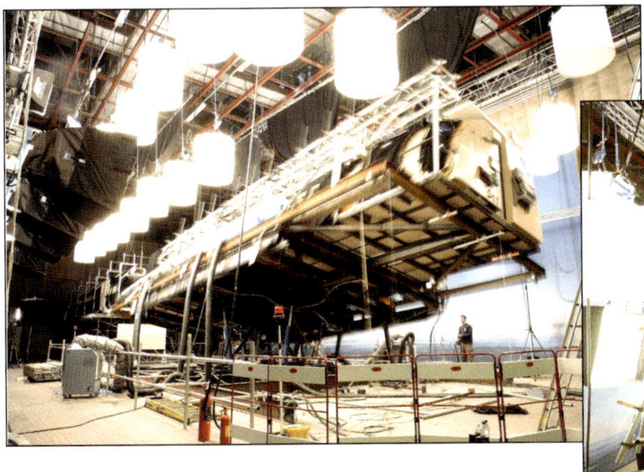

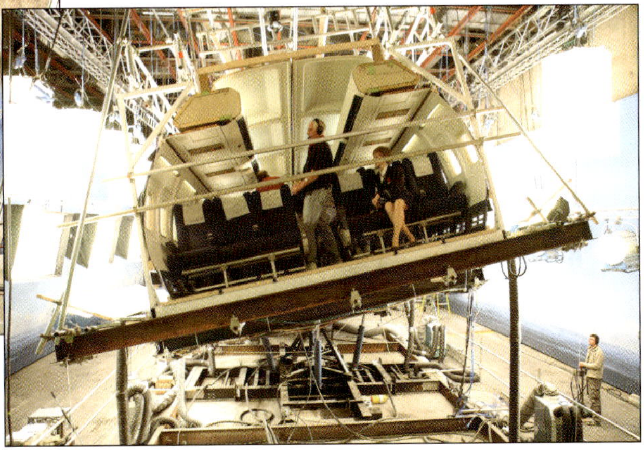

Jonathan Olley

Writer/director/producer Paul Greengrass with the cast and crew.

Q & A

Q: How did the project for *United 93* start?

Paul Greengrass: Quickly. [Producer Lloyd Levin and I] were chatting one night about what to do next, and we were talking about Flight 93 and how I had always been interested in it, but I wasn't sure it was the right time. And we talked about the Discovery thing [a Discovery Channel docudrama about the flight], so I knew that was sort of coming down. I was talking to Lloyd about why I felt that if I made something now, 9/11 was something I would like to address. I talked about Flight 93 in terms of it giving you an extraordinary way into 9/11. He just said, "You should make it. You really should." And I thought, "You know what? He's right."

So I decided to write something. I put aside a week to write something and see if what comes out can express the things that I think and feel about it. Which is what I did.

Q: A lot of people are saying that it's still too soon for this kind of a film. What's your response to that?

PG: I think in the end that movies are the principal means of mass-communication. They're the principal way that we tell stories about the way we're living to each other. We tell stories to entertain ourselves, and to divert ourselves, and we tell stories that are wonderful pieces of escapism, to give us a nice time on a rainy day. There are all sorts of reasons why we like to tell stories to tell each other. But one of the things we do is tell stories about the way the world is. I believe in a movie industry that operates across the board—it makes all sorts of different types of films. Including films about the big stuff facing us. Hollywood has always done that, throughout its history. It's always done that, as well as all the other things. And it will have to grapple with 9/11 because it's the single most important event that's occurred in our lifetime.

This interview from "Cinematic Happenings Under Development" (CHUD.com, December 16, 2005) was conducted by Devin Faraci. Two subsequent interviews with Paul Greengrass have been published on the web site. Reprinted by permission.

It was already happening when I was sitting down thinking about doing this. Oliver Stone was doing his, there's *102 Minutes*. You can just feel when it's in the air. I think it's important to do that. I think it's very, very important that we try to understand what happened and what it meant. For me the most important thing about this film is that it's a film about 9/11 that can talk about just that—what happened. In a simple, unvarnished way, without being presented in an excessively fictionalized way. It can just give you the 9/11 experience.

That, in a way, ought to be the starting point. We'll be grappling with and reflecting on 9/11 for years, in many different ways. There will be some fantastic films that will be purely fictional, of all types. A film that just gives you what happens on that day, which is a great place to start.

Q: If you're trying to give us just what happened that day, United 93 is an interesting place to start, since there are things that we do know about that flight, but we have no idea about many of the details. There's a lot we really don't know. How do you handle that?

PG: What you do is that you start with the story on the ground. That is as important as the story of what happened in the air, because the story on the ground is about the civilian air traffic control system and the military air traffic control system faced with, out of the clear blue sky, the most unimaginable and unimagined crisis. First one, then two, then three, then four planes—at that point they thought up to a dozen had been hijacked and were flying around, undetectable, heading God knows where.

That is a story which you can know to be absolute last detail how that played out. The grappling for information between the civilian system and the military system. The difficulties they had dealing with what they were dealing with. In effect what they were dealing with was a new world while they were still in the old one. What you have to do is put the building blocks of that in place so that you understand Flight 93 in its true context, that it was the last airplane.

What's really interesting is that when you look at it like that, you realize something important about Flight 93, which is that it, in many ways, occurred in the post-9/11 world because of the quirk of fate that that airplane was delayed on the ground for forty-five minutes. Not long after it was airborne, the first two planes went into the World Trade Center. By the time

Flight 93 was hijacked, the third plane had practically gone into the Pentagon.

What it means is that you had forty people—or slightly less, as some had been killed—essentially you had a small number of people on an airplane who were the first people to inhabit the post-9/11 world. For all the rest of us, whether we were in civilian air traffic control, Presidential bunkers, or just ordinary folks like us watching on TV, we knew something terrible was happening, but we didn't really know what. We maybe knew it was terrorism, but we didn't know what. But for those people on the airplane they knew exactly what it was, they could see what was facing them, and here's the thing—they faced a terrible, terrible dilemma. The dilemma was: what do we do? Do we sit here and hope for the best? Or do we strike back at them before they do what we think they might be about to do? In the course of action of whatever those two choices we make, what are the chances of a good outcome from either of those two choices?

That dilemma is the post-9/11 dilemma. It's the dilemma we have all faced since then. The things we face in our world—whether it's Afghanistan or Iraq or Abu Ghraib, issues of world peace, issues of national security, it doesn't matter. And it doesn't matter where you are on the political spectrum and how you view those issues. I would submit that all of us, whatever our persuasions are, all of us understand that that is the dilemma. What do we do? How do we deal with this thing?

To answer your question, we know from the fragments that we can from the airplane—the phone calls, the cockpit voice recorders, the evidence we can deduce from the other planes—we know they weighed, they debated the issue. They voted on it. In the end they acted, and there were consequences. I think that if you build this film up on a strong foundation of fact, that by the time you get to the last minutes of that airplane journey you'll be inhabiting a debate that, whilst we cannot know exactly what it was, we know broadly how it goes—because it's our debate now.

If you get 44 actors, and you get them to inhabit that situation, I believe you can get that truth—you really do.

Q: You're filming this on a small airplane set with all of these actors, and it's such a heavy story—what's the mood like from day to day?

PG: Fantastically disciplined and committed, I would say. I think people share that view that we need to address 9/11, and that's what we're here to do. What you have to do is be cool and disciplined and dispassionate and level-headed. Otherwise it becomes an exercise in simple emotionality. We have got to get to some of the truths of this thing in a simple way. Actors are fantastically good at doing that. They have the ability to show you things so that you can say, "Well, it must have been like that."

Q: One of the interesting differences between your film and Oliver Stone's film is that he's chosen a story with a happy ending. He has the two guys coming out of the rubble at the end. Yours ends tragically.

PG: Listen, I think *United 93* is an unbelievably inspiring story. You're talking about exceptional courage. You're talking about being at the heart of our world today. Thought-provoking, yes, but you're never going to make a story out of 9/11 and turn it into a happy ending truly, are you? Otherwise what are we saying here?

9/11, no matter where you are on the political spectrum, changed our world. It forced us to confront the way our world is going, and it presented us with some hard choices. That's what a film needs to do, help us understand some of those things, but also of course take us to the heart of the human stories.

PRODUCTION NOTES

> *There are lots of ways to find meaning in the events of 9/11. Television can convey events as they happen. A reporter can write history's rough first draft. Historians can widen the time frame and give us context…Filmmakers have a part to play, too, and I believe that sometimes, if you look clearly and unflinchingly at a single event, you can find in its shape something much larger than the event itself—the DNA of our times…Hence a film about United 93.*
>
> —Paul Greengrass

Paul Greengrass has spent the larger part of his career crafting socially aware, humane films about some of the thorniest issues of our modern day—the flashpoint at which politics turn to violence, beliefs slip into zealotry—in addition to helming an international blockbuster thriller, 2004's *The Bourne Supremacy*.

He is perhaps best remembered for his critically acclaimed cinéma vérité exploration of the 1972 incident in Londonderry, Northern Ireland, when thirteen unarmed civil rights demonstrators were shot by British soldiers—2002's visceral drama *Bloody Sunday*. In his review of the film, *Los Angeles Times* critic Kenneth Turan called it "a compelling, gut-clutching piece of advocacy cinema that carries you along in a torrent of emotion as it explores the awful complications of one terrifying day. *Bloody Sunday* shows the power of real events dramatically conveyed. Made by writer-director Paul Greengrass out of a sense of communal outrage that has not gone away, this film never wavers, never loses its focus or its conviction. *Bloody Sunday* does the spirit of that awful day full and unforgettable justice."

Greengrass is, therefore, uniquely qualified to tackle a film that concerns the events that occurred on September 11, 2001, possessing both sensitivity to the subject matter (and its larger themes) and the cinematic talent to handle such a project (with its multiple story threads and constantly shifting viewpoint). Since that autumn day nearly five years ago, the filmmaker has been intent upon telling a story of the epochal events of 9/11, with the question being, "At what point is it okay to put such a painful time on the screen?"

According to Greengrass—informed with interviews from more than one hundred family members and friends of the forty fallen passengers and crew—the right time is when the families say, "Yes."

Greengrass says, "There are all sorts of films made. We make films to divert us, to entertain us and to make us laugh—to take us to fantasy worlds and to make us understand love. But also, there's a place for films that explore the way the world is. And Hollywood has a long and honorable track record of making those types of films as well."

What Greengrass believes is that in examining the story of United 93, we see, in shocking microcosm and within the span of a mere half-hour, the challenges that now face our world as a whole. He continues, "Forty ordinary people had thirty minutes to confront the reality of the way that we're living now, decide on the best course of action and act. They were the first people to inhabit the post 9/11 world—at a time when the rest of us were watching television dumbstruck, unable to understand what was going on. At that moment, those people onboard that airplane knew very well—they could see exactly what they were dealing with—and were faced with a dreadful choice. Do we sit here and do nothing and hope for the best, hope it turns out all right? Or do we do something about it? And if so, what can we do?

"It seems to me that those are the two choices that face us today and have faced us ever since that day. When you look at what happened on that airplane, you can see that there was a debate, an anguished debate in the most terrible of circumstances. That group of people weighed those choices, made a decision and acted upon it. And I think that if we look at what happened, we find a story of immense courage and fortitude—those people were very, very brave. But we also find wisdom."

With regard to the timing of a motion picture about 9/11, Allison Vadhan, daughter of UA 93 passenger Kristin White Gould, offers, "It's never going to be over for us families who've lost loved ones. It's never going to be over for the country, anyone who witnessed it on TV. It's always going to be touchy, awkward…and something that a part of us don't want to see again. But I feel the more films, the better. We can't forget. We have to remember what happened, why it happened. And we can't fool ourselves into thinking that it won't happen again if we forget about it."

Sandy Felt, who lost husband Edward P. Felt on the flight, explains, "There are lots of things in life that are difficult to do, and we do them because they're the right thing to do. This is one of those situations—I got involved in this because it was the right thing to do. I can't deny its existence. I don't know that it's going to be any different for me a year from now, two years from now—it's happened, we deal with it. So I'd rather give you the story, and I'd rather remember the man that he was and be able to keep him alive for myself that way."

Kenny Nacke, brother of passenger Louis J. Nacke, II, shares, "I'm glad it's being made because it's the fifth-year anniversary of it—and I would hate to see those forty individuals forgotten. What if roles were reversed? I've done that, I've said, 'Well, what if I was on Flight 93, and my brother was here today?' And that's why I'm involved. I think he would have the loudest voice. He would say, 'These individuals need to be honored, cherished and remembered.' And I'm going do my part to see that they are, and they're given the credit that they're due—not only for who they were, but what they did that day."

GENESIS OF THE FILM

Well before his contact with the families had bolstered Greengrass' intention to make a 9/11 film, the writer/director had been vigilantly following the media's coverage of the day and its aftermath. After the completion of *The Bourne Supremacy* and the interruption of a subsequent studio project, the filmmaker's thoughts about making the film returned. Yet, he thought, "I wasn't sure it was the right time."

He discussed his idea with producer Lloyd Levin: to use United 93 as a focal point, a prism through which to view the events of the day, to give the audience "an extraordinary way into 9/11." Greengrass then sat down and, drawing on his previous work and research, composed a document that included his feelings and ideas about the project, which eventually became a twenty-one-page treatment. Completed, it contained his reasons for making the film, as well as a time-coded, scene-by-scene plot, telling the general story of the morning as viewed by those in the flight towers and centers on the ground and those aboard the plane itself. This, in turn, was used to pitch the project; eventually, production and distribution deals were secured in the summer of 2005.

Greengrass' aim to keep the story among the flight controllers and the flight's passengers and crew was intentional. Quoting from the treatment, he says, "It's not a film with neat character arcs. What it does do is pick up forty-four individuals as they congregate at the airport for a plane journey, follow them as they enter the plane, and take their ninety-minute journey in real time, cutting away only to the various air traffic control centers that follow their progress, on whose screens the entire horror of the full 9/11 operation is played out."

In August, Greengrass tapped associate Kate Solomon to act as researcher and family liaison. Solomon began by sending a letter to all of the families of United 93's passengers and crew. In the letter, Greengrass' goals for the project were discussed, and he asked for their cooperation in helping to establish profiles of all of those onboard. Ultimately, nearly all of the families participated in the process. What followed in September and October was seven weeks of face-to-face interviews with the families and friends—more than one hundred were conducted in all.

Solomon provides, "They wished to be involved, to honor and remember their loved ones. It's still a painful subject, but many felt that their involvement would help us get it right."

The families were also kept involved all through production of *United 93*. They were notified once casting had been completed and were sent a full cast list and a cast picture of the actors who would portray their family members—some of the actors personally met with the families, while others got in touch on the phone. Solomon also sent out bi-weekly newsletters, which kept them informed of the production's progress and brought them inside the filming process with articles about Greengrass' methods of filming and things like set construction, sound recording and other aspects of moviemaking. The director also recorded a video message for the families that was viewable in a privately accessible area of the web site. The result was an open channel of communication between filmmakers and families, which not only kept all mindful of the film's goals, but also allowed for an ongoing exchange of information. ("Some of the families have taken to calling it 'our film,'" Solomon adds.)

To cover the ground personnel who paid witness to the unfolding tragedy that September day, Greengrass enlisted writer and former *60 Minutes II* producer Michael Bronner to conduct a second series of interviews—this time with a wide-ranging group of civilian and military personnel. As the big picture of the day only began to come clear once geographically dispersed puzzle pieces were assembled, Greengrass knew his narrative would include sequences in several key sites: the control tower at Newark International Airport (where UA Flight 93 originated and which, because of its location, provides a bird's-eye view of Manhattan); Control Centers in Boston (where the hijacked AA Flights 11 and 175 originated) and New York; the Federal Aviation Administration's operations command center in Herndon, Virginia (under the command of national operations manager Ben Sliney, experiencing his first day in that position on 9/11/01); and the military's operations center at the Northeast Air Defense Sector (N.E.A.D.S.) in upstate New York. Bronner's detailed recounting of the events that morning would play a major part in the construction of Greengrass' script.

Additionally, Bronner researched other factual information on everything from the hijackers to the other planes (commercial, military and private) in the air that morning. Valuable information was also gained from the 9/11 Commission Report; members of that Commission advised on the film prior to the start of principal photography and were present on the set during filming.

Greengrass explains, "What we did on this film was to gather together an extraordinary array of people wanting to get this film right—aircrew from United Airlines; pilots; the families of the people who were onboard, who gave us their sense of what their family member might have done given the type of person he or she was in any given situation; controllers and members of the military; the 9/11 Commission. We had a lot of expertise that, in the end, allows you to get a good sense of the general shape of events."

CASTING

Casting was handled primarily out of New York City, with calls going out not only for those actors who resembled the actual people aboard the flight, but also for any performers who may have flight-related experience that could be germane to the characters. Actors who made it to audition found that Greengrass' unusual working style was apparent right from the start—no scripts (or "sides") were provided, and actors were brought into the room in groups, instead of one at a time. Once inside, they were given minimal information, only that the film concerned United 93. Chairs were arranged in rows, as on a plane, and the group was then instructed to improv (e.g., getting on the plane, reacting to a hijacker).

Actor David Rasche, eventually cast as passenger Donald Freeman Greene, remembers, "The audition process was very mysterious—they just said that it was about United 93, that was it. It was really interesting to see people going through various stages of hysteria or however they reacted to the situation. Then they said, 'Thank you.' That was it." Of the entire audition and filming process, Rasche adds, "Paul has more courage about diving into the complete unknown than (any director) I've ever been involved with. The most difficult thing for me was the convergence of realities—the reality of what Paul thinks happened, then what I think happened…but the truth is no one knows for sure. It was a challenge and a fascinating work experience."

For a director looking to create a believable truth, the verisimilitude of the flight personnel's actions necessitated a search within the ranks of actual experienced crew members. Commercial airline pilot JJ Johnson (who has enjoyed a distinguished career with United Airlines) was told about the film by another pilot, who ended up recommending Johnson for the role. Next thing he knew, Johnson received a call from a casting agent, who wanted to know how quickly he could be in New York for an interview—in his captain's uniform; Johnson was later cast as UAL 93's Captain Jason M. Dahl. Johnson arranged for the five weeks off from United, noting, "They were very supportive of me."

The role of First Officer LeRoy Homer was filled by Gary Commock, who has flown commercially (passengers and freight) for just over a decade. (Both Johnson and Commock—in the course of their work—flew commercial 747s to arrive in London just prior to arriving on the *United 93* set.) Of the five flight attendants on United 93, two—Sandra Bradshaw and Lorraine G. Bay—were played by actresses who had worked as United flight attendants: Trish Gates (still working in the field when cast) and Nancy

McDoniel. Their experience proved invaluable to the other actors, particularly those cast as the three additional flight attendants, who would look to them for advice on in-flight procedures.

Other roles were also filled by those best equipped for the characters—civilian and military controllers (some of whom had been on duty on 9/11) were interspersed among actors on the sets of the Newark tower, as well as the Herndon, N.E.A.D.S., Boston, New York and Cleveland centers. Real-life Boston controller Thomas "Tommy" Roberts; military specialist Colin Scoggins; and N.E.A.D.S.' Major James Fox, Senior Director, Weapons Crew and First Lieutenant Jeremy Powell, Senior Director, Technician, were among those who participated, replaying before the cameras the events they themselves had witnessed firsthand nearly five years ago.

The FAA's Ben Sliney had initially signed on to work in an advisory capacity. His nearly three decades of expertise in air traffic control and singular involvement with the events of 9/11 (as the man in charge of the FAA's command center in Herndon) would render him a highly valued asset to Greengrass and his team. He was then invited to work on-camera during filming, portraying a controller in the New York center. Ultimately, he was asked to step into the shoes of one of the key players of the day—so Ben Sliney was eventually cast as Ben Sliney.

The FAA center in Herndon is a unique facility in that it does not communicate directly with aircraft. Instead, it exercises command authority over the twenty regional air traffic control facilities in the United States, overriding those regional boundaries and facilitating cooperation among the separate entities when the situation calls. On the morning of September 11, it fell to Sliney to give the order to clear the skies, landing approximately 4,500 commercial and general aviation aircraft within hours, before any more could become involved (at one point, it was believed as many as eleven planes had been hijacked). Astoundingly, this was accomplished without further incident…and all of this on Sliney's first day at the job.

Relating his experience reliving 9/11 for the cameras, Sliney states, "What I was called upon to do for Paul was accurate, in that I would have responded in the way that he wanted me to—albeit it was heightened for the purposes of the film. But it was factual in the progression of the events, since it was developed using the facts from the 9/11 Commission Report. I cannot say I was nervous, and I attribute that to being relaxed around Paul, knowing that he had provided the parameters of the scene and you had the freedom to bounce around within those. I think also, having read the treatment, it seemed to me that the story was about how people in ordinary walks of life—without any guidance from hierarchy or protocol—could all rise to an occasion, which culminated in the ultimate self-sacrifice of the people on United 93. It was focused and clear, so it was easy to do my job on the set."

Production had also begun searching for another important element that would play a key role in the re-creation of the day: a plane. Fortunately, the production team found a twenty-year-old, out-of-service Boeing 757 earmarked for the scrap heap, had it dismantled and shipped to Pinewood Studios outside of London, where *United 93* would be filmed. Then, gleaning instruction from a massive, 9,600-page "owner's" manual, the production crew began the careful re-assembly of the 140-foot-long fuselage. Rather than putting it back together as one contiguous piece, however, builders reconstructed the 757 in pull-apart sections (the cockpit, first class, and coach cabins). Each could later be mounted separately on motion gimbals that could simulate the movements of the plane (banking, ascending, descending, turbulence), or assembled back in one piece. The art department then performed a makeover on the interior, dressing the seats and cabins with period-appropriate, company-issue graphics, fabrics, lights, magazines, even the correct images on the in-flight television monitors—all to replicate, as closely as possible, the appearance of the five-year-old Boeing 757 that took off from Newark on September 11 and later crashed in a field in Somerset County, Pennsylvania, near the town of Shanksville.

RESEARCH AND FACT GATHERING

The filmmakers' decision to shoot at Pinewood was carefully considered. Greengrass' film would be the product of some improvisation, all based on the known facts, and it was felt that in order for the cast to arrive at their own truths about their characters and the events on the plane, there would need to be a removal from the culture where the impact of 9/11 is still keenly and painfully felt—much as a jury in deliberation is separated from the media and immediate influences of the outside world. During the intense, pre-shoot rehearsal process, as well as during principal photography, a majority of the actors stayed in a hotel near the studio (a few, who were U.K.-based, did return to their homes).

Once they had been signed to their parts, each actor was given a dossier (the product of the researchers and the family input) on the person they would be portraying. These files contained photos, information from the family (What kind of person was he/she?) and practical facts (How did this person get to the airport? What clothing was he/she wearing?). Some of the actors' research processes included their own personal outreach to the family, while some preferred to develop the character simply with the research provided.

There was an acknowledgment—from the actors and the families—of the difficulty of re-creating a real person who, in the final moments of life, had been subjected to an unthinkable ordeal. Both groups were respectful of the burdens and responsibilities of the other and only interacted if the willingness to communicate was shared by all.

Lorna Dallas, cast as passenger Linda Gronlund, exchanged several phone calls with Linda's sister, Elsa, and later met with her and Gronlund's mother, who closed their meeting with a toast to her "new daughter." Dallas says, after given permission to make the call to Elsa, "I felt at that point that I was talking to my own sister. She made me feel very comfortable. We laughed and cried on the phone—she wanted to know about me, and I told her a few things, told her about my background. And then, it started coming out from her, about Linda. And it was just spilling out—the time on the phone didn't matter. The minutes just flew by. I had several phone calls with Elsa, and each time, new things came up."

A trusting bond built, Elsa later shared her sister's last call with the actor. Dallas reflects, "When I heard it, it was rather harrowing and rather humbling to know that someone who knew that the end was very near could have such forethought, such strength to say what she did. She told Elsa exactly where to go for her will. And she ended that phone call with 'I love you.' It took great guts to say what she did on that phone. And it took great guts for Elsa to play it for me…and it will haunt me for the rest of my life. But I will also treasure the thought, and be grateful of the strength of that woman that was shared with me."

Peter Hermann, signed to play passenger Jeremy Glick, comments, "This is incredibly tender territory that's been entrusted to us. I mean, it's an incredible act of trust, as a family member who lost someone on United 93, to give this over, to say, 'Yes, you can portray my husband.' That's a huge thing. And I think it really helped to be isolated as a cast, that we didn't disperse at night…and I don't know what it would have been like to make this movie in the States."

For Cheyenne Jackson, portraying passenger Mark Bingham brought great responsibility and challenges. He explains, "Early on, they gave us the option to contact family members, and I was really torn about that decision. On one hand, it was a great opportunity to talk to the people that knew these people better than anybody. And on the other hand, it seemed rather daunting. I was pretty trepidatious. But, I did decide to reach out via e-mail to Mark's mom, and she was lovely. And it was just what I needed. It was supportive, and it was open—she's a no-nonsense kind of gal, and I really appreciated that. Also I talked to a former partner of his, and also his dad. The whole idea of trying to capture somebody's spirit, somebody's essence, though, has been overwhelming."

Of the phone calls those on United 93 made—like the one from Linda Gronlund to her sister (scripts for which were provided to the actors for use during filming)—Christian Clemenson (who plays passenger Thomas E. Burnett, Jr.) comments, "I've read the transcripts or what people recollect of all the phone calls and what strikes me about all of them is how calm these people were. That is astounding to me. Tolstoy wrote that the aim of art is to state the question clearly—it's not to provide answers. And I think that's what Paul is doing with this movie."

The practical research by both Solomon and Bronner also played a part in the costuming of the film, with history helping to determine what the flight crews on United Airlines planes wore in 2001. The type of person each passenger was (again determined from information provided by the family members) was factored into clothing choices for their characters. And as with the outfitting of the plane, reality was the overriding concern for determining the final clothing looks for all.

Once assembled at Pinewood, the cast who comprised *United 93*'s passengers and crew began their arduous journey together by embarking upon an intensive, two-week rehearsal process. Having digested the background research on their characters, they were now to become those characters involved in a harrowing situation. Much like a stage play (only without a majority of dialogue scripted), the actors would board the plane—the reconstructed, re-dressed Boeing 757—and sit in their assigned seats. The planes' doors would be shut and those aboard would re-enact the ninety-one-minute flight in real time…from takeoff to the descent over Pennsylvania. These improvisations were executed within certain parameters, such as the times of known events (e.g., the mundane first forty-six minutes of the flight, the takeover of the plane, air-to-ground communications) and the "makeup" of their characters (e.g., leader or follower). Times were called out during improv and filming, to give the actors a framework on which to shape their communal drama. Executed repeatedly, with various sequences of the improv revisited over and over during the course of the two weeks, Greengrass' goal of the "plausible truth" began to emerge.

Greengrass explains, "We improvised based on the known events. And all the time we were engaged in a debate about how believable it was. How might a group of young men have reacted in this situation? How might more elderly people on that airplane have reacted? How might the flight attendants have reacted? You know, those are the questions that we discussed and tried to arrive at a workable solution in an improvisatory style."

Olivia Thirlby (playing passenger Nicole Carol Miller) reasons, "Working with improvisation has been appropriate for this project and for this subject matter. We just have no way of knowing the events that happened on the plane. There would be no way to script it in a way that would end up seeming realistic. This is such touchy subject matter—and I think that if it's not going to be truthful and it's not going to seem real, then there's just no point in doing it."

Susan Blommaert (playing passenger Jane Folger) adds, "I feel like Paul is anti-sensationalist and an anti-sentimentalist. It was always about trying to create, as honestly as we possibly can, what could have happened on that plane. There was no pretense to make it anything other than that. I think that has really been inspirational to all of us, and I think the only way that you can feel justified in doing this movie."

Marceline Hugot (playing passenger Georgine Rose Corrigan) offers, "Paul basically wanted us to respect profoundly who we were representing. Learn as much or as little as was available about the person and embody that, making decisions within that framework. It became a marriage between an actor and a person who lived, breathed, had a full life and tragically ended up in a horrible, horrible situation. So it was about trying to re-create that for myself, and then, way beyond...for the family. It's surprising how simple, not simplistic, a process it really is. And to have a director encourage that clarity and simpleness of heart is rare...and I'm hoping the film's as powerful to see as it has been to do."

Greengrass sought to keep the rehearsal process truthful. Since the onboard conflict was literally a deadly contest of "us against them," the director kept the four U.K.-based actors who were cast as the plane's young hijackers separate from the forty passengers and crew—and introduced them as late in the game as he could. These actors had also been provided with factual information about their characters, including the written instructions for their mission from the leader of the 9/11 plot, Mohamed Atta. Additionally, they were given intense, accelerated physical training from martial arts experts.

All through pre-production and rehearsal, Greengrass had been developing a "shooting script" which listed scenes and action. Also, verified dialogue of ground and flight personnel was included. After the culmination of the rehearsal process, the scenes aboard the plane were fleshed out with a great deal of description of the action, but only a few bits of key dialogue—the remainder would be provided during the filmed sequences out of the reality created during on-camera improvisation.

PRINCIPAL PHOTOGRAPHY

Principal photography of *United 93* began in mid-November, on the sets that the actors had come to know very well during the time spent in rehearsal. The first scenes shot involved the entire plane. As previously, the plane was boarded with the doors sealed—and filmed takes varied in duration, from anywhere between a few to as many as forty minutes. Filming was executed by two camera operators who, along with sound men and an assistant director, would run up and down the length of the set at the direction of Greengrass, communicating with them from outside the plane through microphones and earpieces. (The final task of making a seamless film from these different segments would fall to Greengrass and his team of three editors.)

Next, scenes were completed in the separate cabins—first economy, then first-class. The harrowing last minutes fighting for control of the plane were shot separately, with the cockpit fixed to a computer-controlled hydraulic gimbal—designed in cooperation with the special effects department—which pitched and rolled in simulation of a plane spiraling out of control.

Even with all of the rehearsal, scenarios and objectives still continued to be refined. Peter Hermann remembers a take at the end of a full day: "By the time that we'd got to shooting the final scenes in that contained space, we were incredibly tired and there was a lot of accumulated adrenaline. I think that, in a sense, it's those moments that become a real luxury, because the objective is so clear: get in that door, and get anybody who's in the way *out* of the way. It just becomes so basic and so clear."

The first-class section was later fitted into a rotating gimbal, which could turn the cabin 180 degrees during the filming of the final scenes, as the plane is making its last (and very steep) dive. To lessen the chances of injury, the seat frames, backs and armrests were refitted with soft foam in place of the hard plastic and metal. Stunt performers were originally intended to stand in for the cast in these scenes, but the actors wished to execute the work themselves. With extra padding built into their costumes, they successfully completed their own stunts.

Greengrass observes, "That final image haunts me—a physical struggle for the controls of a gasoline-fueled twenty-first-century flying machine between a band of suicidal religious fanatics and a group of innocents drawn at random from amongst us all…I think of it often. It's really, in a way, the struggle for our world today."

On the filming of the final sequences between the hijackers and the hijacked, Kate Jennings Grant (playing passenger Lauren Catuzzi Grandcolas) observes, "It was astounding to me that as actors (and we know what's going to happen), there was still something in us that was also in those passengers: the undeniably human—and I'd like to think American—urge to cling to hope. You cling and you fight because life is extraordinary. One life is extraordinary and worth it. In those moments where I started to collapse from exhaustion crawling up that aisle, I would think of Lauren, and I would think of my family and all those I would be flying home to…and I kept going and going and going."

Filming on the sets of the control centers and towers was given the same attention to improvisational truth and detail—all executed within the parameters of actual timing and known fact. Whether Greengrass' cameras were focused on one screen, one individual or the entire facility, all actors were engaged, performing and reacting in every take—even if what they did was clearly out of frame.

Sometimes, the convergence of the filmic world and the real world proved to be a near overwhelming experience for those involved. As a real-life flight attendant for United, Trish Gates had been pulled from her original assignment to work a Newark/Los Angeles flight two days before September 11. The day prior, she had worked a trip up to Portland, where she was grounded for five days following. She remembered a poster that showed the faces of the crew members killed on September 11—in particular, the face of Sandra Bradshaw, the woman she was cast to portray. Gates tells, "The first two weeks of rehearsal, I was busy trying to make sure that everything looked real and that all of the attendants were doing the right thing. Then, I felt the responsibility that she was an actual person the day we started shooting—it hit me. I looked again at all the information and the pictures, and I felt this enormous responsibility to do right by her…to do the best job that I could. Before every take, I would look at this little family portrait and think about her children—the youngest one doesn't have a memory of her, and that just broke my heart."

It is that very convergence of realities—resulting in a communally discovered truth—that compels Paul Greengrass to make films like *United 93*. He closes, "I hope that people see that this film has been made in a serious way by serious people trying to do a difficult thing, which is to explore a very painful event—and that it's been done in a dignified way and that what we present is a believable truth. If we do that, well, I will feel that we've done as best we can. September 11, no matter where you are on the political spectrum, changed our world. It forced us to confront the way our world is going, and it presented us with some hard choices. That's what a film needs to do, to help us understand some of those things…but also, of course, to take us to the heart of the human stories of those involved."

9/11 LIVE: THE NORAD TAPES

MICHAEL BRONNER

Former 60 Minutes II producer and writer Michael Bronner was enlisted by Paul Greengrass to conduct interviews with and do research on a wide-ranging group of civilian and military personnel connected with UA Flight 93 to help construct an accurate script. The following detailed account is from the military's operations center at the Northeast Air Defense Sector (N.E.A.D.S.) in upstate New York.

Tucked in a piney notch in the gentle folds of the Adirondacks' southern skirts—just up from a derelict Mohawk, Adirondack & Northern rail spur—is a 22-year-old aluminum bunker tricked out with antennae tilted skyward. It could pass for the Jetsons' garage or, in the estimation of one of the higher-ranking U.S. Air Force officers stationed there, a big, sideways, half-buried beer keg.

As Major Kevin Nasypany, the facility's mission-crew commander, drove up the hill to work on the morning of 9/11, he was dressed in his flight suit and prepared for battle. Not a real one. The Northeast Air Defense Sector (NEADS), where Nasypany had been stationed since 1994, is the regional headquarters for the North American Aerospace Defense Command (NORAD), the Cold War–era military organization charged with protecting North American airspace. As he poured his first coffee on that sunny September morning, the odds that he would have to defend against Russian "Bear Bombers," one of NORAD's traditional simulated missions, were slim. Rather, Nasypany (pronounced Nah-*sip*-a-nee), an amiable commander with a thick mini-mustache and a hockey player's build, was headed in early to get ready for the NORAD-wide training exercise he'd helped design. The battle commander, Colonel Bob Marr, had promised to bring in fritters.

Michael Bronner was an associate producer on the movie *United 93*. This article originally appeared in the August 2006 issue of *Vanity Fair*. Reprinted by permission.

NEADS is a desolate place, the sole orphan left behind after the dismantling of what was once one of the country's busiest bomber bases—Griffiss Air Force Base, in Rome, New York, which was otherwise mothballed in the mid-90s. NEADS's mission remained in place and continues today: its officers, air-traffic controllers, and air-surveillance and communications technicians—mostly American, with a handful of Canadian troops—are responsible for protecting a half-million-square-mile chunk of American airspace stretching from the East Coast to Tennessee, up through the Dakotas to the Canadian border, including Boston, New York, Washington, D.C., and Chicago.

It was into this airspace that violence descended on 9/11, and from the NEADS operations floor that what turned out to be the sum total of America's military response during those critical 100-some minutes of the attack—scrambling four armed fighter jets and one unarmed training plane—emanated.

The story of what happened in that room, and when, has never been fully told, but is arguably more important in terms of understanding America's military capabilities that day than anything happening simultaneously on Air Force One or in the Pentagon, the White House, or NORAD's impregnable headquarters, deep within Cheyenne Mountain, in Colorado. It's a story that was intentionally obscured, some members of the 9/11 commission believe, by military higher-ups and members of the Bush administration who spoke to the press, and later the commission itself, in order to downplay the extent of the confusion and miscommunication flying through the ranks of the government.

The truth, however, is all on tape.

Through the heat of the attack the wheels of what were, perhaps, some of the more modern pieces of equipment in the room—four Dictaphone multi-channel reel-to-reel tape recorders mounted on a rack in a corner of the operations floor—spun impassively, recording every radio channel, with time stamps.

The recordings are fascinating and chilling. A mix of staccato bursts of military code; urgent, overlapping voices; the tense crackle of radio traffic from fighter pilots in the air; commanders' orders piercing through a mounting din; and candid moments of emotion as the breadth of the attacks becomes clearer.

For the NEADS crew, 9/11 was not a story of four hijacked airplanes, but one of a heated chase after more than a dozen potential hijackings—some real, some phantom—that emerged from the turbulence of misinformation that spiked in the first 100 minutes of the attack and continued well into the afternoon and evening. At one point, in the span of a single mad minute, one hears Nasypany struggling to parse reports of four separate hijackings at once. What emerges from the barrage of what Nasypany dubs "bad poop" flying at his troops from all directions is a picture of remarkable composure. Snap decisions more often than not turn out to be the right ones as commanders kick-start the dormant military machine. It is the fog and friction of war live—the authentic military history of 9/11.

"The real story is actually better than the one we told," a NORAD general admitted to 9/11-commission staffers when confronted with evidence from the tapes that contradicted his original testimony. And so it seems.

Subpoenaed by the commission during its investigation, the recordings have never been played publicly beyond a handful of sound bites presented during the commission's hearings. Last September, as part of my research for the film *United 93,* on which I was an associate producer, I requested copies from the Pentagon. I was played snippets, but told my chances of hearing the full recordings were nonexistent. So it was a surprise, to say the least, when a military public-affairs officer e-mailed me, a full seven months later, saying she'd been cleared, finally, to provide them.

"The signing of the Declaration of Independence took less coordination," she wrote.

I would ultimately get three CDs with huge digital "wav file" recordings of the various channels in each section of the operations floor, 30-some hours of material in full, covering six and a half hours of real time. The first disc, which arrived by mail, was decorated with blue sky and fluffy white clouds and was labeled, in the playful Apple Chancery font, "Northeast Air Defense Sector—DAT Audio Files—11 Sep 2001."

"THIS IS NOT AN EXERCISE"

At 8:14 a.m., as an Egyptian and four Saudis commandeered the cockpit on American 11, the plane that would hit the north tower of the World Trade Center, only a handful of troops were on the NEADS "ops" floor. That's the facility's war room: a dimly lit den arrayed with long rows of radarscopes and communications equipment facing a series of 15-foot screens lining the front wall. The rest of the crew, about 30 Americans and five or six Canadians, were checking e-mails or milling around the hall. A briefing on the morning's training exercise was wrapping up in the Battle Cab, the glassed-in command area overlooking the ops floor.

On the Dictaphone decks, an automated voice on each channel ticked off, in Greenwich Mean Time, the last few moments of life in pre-9/11 America: "12 hours, 26 minutes, 20 seconds"—just before 8:30 a.m. eastern daylight time.

The first human voices captured on tape that morning are those of the "ID techs"—Senior Airman Stacia Rountree, 23 at the time, Tech Sergeant Shelley Watson, 40, and their boss, Master Sergeant Maureen "Mo" Dooley, 40. They are stationed in the back right corner of the ops floor at a console with several phones and a radarscope. Their job in a crisis is to facilitate communications between NEADS, the civilian F.A.A., and other military commands, gathering whatever information they can and sending it up the chain. Dooley—her personality at once motherly and aggressive—generally stands behind the other two, who are seated.

The tapes catch them discussing strategy of an entirely domestic order:

08:37:08 *Okay, a couch, an ottoman, a love seat, and what else … ? Was it on sale … ? Holy smokes! What color is it?*

In the background, however, you can make out the sound of Jeremy Powell, then 31, a burly, amiable technical sergeant, fielding the phone call that will be the military's first notification that something is wrong. On the line is Boston Center, the civilian air-traffic-control facility that handles that region's high-flying airliners.

08:37:52 BOSTON CENTER: *Hi. Boston Center T.M.U. [Traffic Management Unit], we have a problem here. We have a hijacked aircraft headed towards New York, and we need you guys to, we need someone to scramble some F-16s or something up there, help us out.*

POWELL: *Is this real-world or exercise?*

BOSTON CENTER: *No, this is not an exercise, not a test.*

Powell's question—"Is this real-world or exercise?"—is heard nearly verbatim over and over on the tapes as troops funnel onto the ops floor and are briefed about the hijacking. Powell, like almost everyone in the room, first assumes the phone call is from the simulations team on hand to send "inputs"—simulated scenarios—into play for the day's training exercise.

Boston's request for fighter jets is not as prescient as it might seem. Standard hijack protocol calls for fighters to be launched—"scrambled"—merely to establish a presence in the air. The pilots are trained to trail the hijacked plane at a distance of about five miles, out of sight, following it until, presumably, it lands. If necessary, they can show themselves, flying up close to establish visual contact, and, if the situation demands, maneuver to force the plane to land.

At this point, certainly, the notion of actually firing anything at a passenger jet hasn't crossed anyone's mind.

In the ID section, the women overhear the word "hijack" and react, innocently enough, as anyone might with news of something exciting going on at work:

8:37:56 WATSON: *What?*

DOOLEY: *Whoa!*

WATSON: *What was that?*

ROUNTREE: *Is that real-world?*

DOOLEY: *Real-world hijack.*

WATSON: *Cool!*

For the first time in their careers, they'll get to put their training to full use.

Almost simultaneously, a P.A. announcement goes out for Major Nasypany, who's taking his morning constitutional.

08:37:58 P.A.: *Major Nasypany, you're needed in ops pronto. Major Nasypany, you're needed in ops pronto.*

[Recorded phone line:] SERGEANT McCAIN: *Northeast Air Defense Sector, Sergeant McCain, can I help you?*

SERGEANT KELLY: *Yeah, Sergeant Kelly from Otis, how you doing today?*

SERGEANT McCAIN: *Yeah, go ahead.*

SERGEANT KELLY: *The—I'm gettin' reports from my TRACON [local civilian air traffic] that there might be a possible hijacking.*

SERGEANT McCAIN: *I was just hearing the same thing. We're workin' it right now.*

SERGEANT KELLY: *Okay, thanks.*

"When they told me there was a hijack, my first reaction was 'Somebody started the exercise early,'" Nasypany later told me. The day's exercise was designed to run a range of scenarios, including a "traditional" simulated hijack in which politically motivated perpetrators commandeer an aircraft, land on a Cuba-like island, and seek asylum. "I actually said out loud, 'The hijack's not supposed to be for another hour,'" Nasypany recalled. (The fact that there was an exercise planned for the same day as the attack factors into several conspiracy theories, though the 9/11 commission dismisses this as coincidence. After plodding through dozens of hours of recordings, so do I.)

On tape, one hears as Nasypany, following standard hijack protocol, prepares to launch two fighters from Otis Air National Guard Base, on Cape Cod, to look for American 11, which is now off course and headed south. He orders his Weapons Team—the group on the ops floor that controls the fighters—to put the Otis planes on "battle stations." This means that at the air base the designated "alert" pilots—two in this case—are jolted into action by a piercing "battle horn." They run to their jets, climb up, strap in, and do everything they need to do to get ready to fly, short of starting the engines.

Meanwhile, the communications team at NEADS—the ID techs Dooley, Rountree, and Watson—are trying to find out, as fast as possible, everything they can about the hijacked plane: the airline, the flight number, the tail number (to help fighter pilots identify it in the air), its flight plan, the number of passengers ("souls on board" in military parlance), and, most important, where it is, so Nasypany can launch the fighters. All the ID section knows is that the plane is American Airlines, Flight No. 11, Boston to Los Angeles, currently somewhere north of John F. Kennedy International Airport—the point of reference used by civilian controllers.

ID tech Watson places a call to the management desk at Boston Center, which first alerted NEADS to the hijack, and gets distressing news.

08:39:58 WATSON: *It's the inbound to J.F.K.?*

BOSTON CENTER: *We—we don't know.*

WATSON: *You don't know where he is at all?*

BOSTON CENTER: *He's being hijacked. The pilot's having a hard time talking to the—I mean, we don't know. We don't know where he's goin'. He's heading towards*

Kennedy. He's—like I said, he's like 35 miles north of Kennedy now at 367 knots. We have no idea where he's goin' or what his intentions are.

WATSON: *If you could* please *give us a call and let us know—you know any information, that'd be great.*

BOSTON CENTER: *Okay. Right now, I guess we're trying to work on—I guess there's been some threats in the cockpit. The pilot—*

WATSON: *There's been what?! I'm sorry.*

UNIDENTIFIED VOICE: *Threat to the … ?*

BOSTON CENTER: *We'll call you right back as soon as we know more info.*

Dooley is standing over Watson, shouting whatever pertinent information she hears to Nasypany, who's now in position in the center of the floor.

08:40:36 DOOLEY: *Okay, he said threat to the cockpit!*

This last bit ratchets the tension in the room up considerably.

At Otis Air National Guard Base, the pilots are in their jets, straining at the reins. ("When the horn goes off, it definitely gets your heart," F-15 pilot Major Dan Nash later told me, thumping his chest with his hand.) But at NEADS, Nasypany's "tracker techs" in the Surveillance section still can't find American 11 on their scopes. As it turns out, this is just as the hijackers intended.

Radar is the NEADS controllers' most vital piece of equipment, but by 9/11 the scopes were so old, among other factors, that controllers were ultimately unable to find any of the hijacked planes in enough time to react. Known collectively as the Green Eye for the glow the radar rings give off, the scopes looked like something out of *Dr. Strangelove* and were strikingly anachronistic compared with the equipment at civilian air-traffic sites. (After 9/11, NEADS was equipped with state-of-the-art equipment.)

In order to find a hijacked airliner—or any airplane—military controllers need either the plane's beacon code (broadcast from an electronic transponder on board) or the plane's exact coordinates. When the hijackers on American 11 turned the beacon off, intentionally losing themselves in the dense sea of airplanes already flying over the U.S. that morning (a tactic that would be repeated, with some variations, on all the hijacked flights), the NEADS controllers were at a loss.

"You would see thousands of green blips on your scope," Nasypany told me, "and now you have to pick and choose. Which is the bad guy out there? Which is the hijacked aircraft? And without that information from F.A.A., it's a needle in a haystack."

At this point in the morning, more than 3,000 jetliners are already in the air over the continental United States, and the Boston controller's direction—"35 miles north of Kennedy"—doesn't help the NEADS controllers at all.

On tape, amid the confusion, one hears Major James Fox, then 32, the leader of the Weapons Team, whose composure will stand out throughout the attack, make an observation that, so far, ranks as the understatement of the morning.

08:43:06 FOX: *I've never seen so much real-world stuff happen during an exercise.*

Less than two minutes later, frustrated that the controllers still can't pinpoint American 11 on radar, Nasypany orders Fox to launch the Otis fighters anyway.

08:44:59 FOX: *M.C.C. [Mission Crew Commander], I don't know where I'm scrambling these guys to. I need a direction, a destination—*

NASYPANY: *Okay, I'm gonna give you the Z point [coordinate]. It's just north of—New York City.*

FOX: *I got this lat long, 41-15, 74-36, or 73-46.*

NASYPANY: *Head 'em in that direction.*

FOX: *Copy that.*

Having them up, Nasypany figures, is better than having them on the ground, assuming NEADS will ultimately pin down American 11's position. His job is to be proactive—to try to gain leverage over the situation as fast as possible. His backstop is Colonel Marr, the battle commander and Nasypany's superior up in the Battle Cab, whose role is more strategic, calculating the implications of each move several hours down the line.

Marr, 48 at the time (and since retired), is a well-liked leader. Most of his conversations on 9/11 are unrecorded: he speaks over a secure phone with his superior, Major General Larry Arnold, stationed at NORAD's command center at Tyndall Air Force Base, in Florida, or over an intercom with

Nasypany. In the latter case, only Nasypany's side of the conversations is recorded.

In the last lines of his first briefing to Marr, Nasypany unwittingly, in his last line, trumps Fox in the realm of understatement.

> 08:46:36 NASYPANY: *Hi, sir. Okay, what—what we're doing, we're tryin' to locate this guy. We can't find him via I.F.F. [the Identification Friend or Foe system]. What we're gonna do, we're gonna hit up every track within a 25-mile radius of this Z-point [coordinate] that we put on the scope. Twenty-nine thousand [feet] heading 1-9-0 [east]. We're just gonna do—we're gonna try to find this guy. They can't find him. There's supposedly been threats to the cockpit. So we're just doing the thing … [off-mic conversation] True. And probably right now with what's going on in the cockpit it's probably really crazy. So, it probably needs to—that will simmer down and we'll probably get some better information.*

American 11 slammed into the north tower of the World Trade Center four seconds into this transmission.

More than 150 miles from Manhattan, within the same minute as American 11 hits the tower, the stoplight in the Alert Barn at Otis Air National Guard Base on Cape Cod turns from red to green, Colonel Marr and General Arnold having approved Nasypany's order to scramble the fighters. The pilots taxi out and fire the afterburners as the planes swing onto the runway. NEADS has no indication yet that American 11 has crashed.

Five minutes later, Rountree, at the ID station, gets the first report of the crash from Boston Center (as her colleagues Watson and Dooley overhear).

> 08:51:11 ROUNTREE: *A plane just hit the World Trade Center.*
>
> WATSON: *What?*
>
> ROUNTREE: *Was it a 737?*
>
> UNIDENTIFIED MALE (background): *Hit what?*
>
> WATSON: *The World Trade Center—*
>
> DOOLEY: *Who are you talking to?* [Gasps.]
>
> WATSON: *Oh!*
>
> DOOLEY: *Get—pass—pass it to them—*
>
> WATSON: *Oh my God. Oh God. Oh my God.*

ROUNTREE: *Saw it on the news. It's—a plane just crashed into the World Trade Center.*

DOOLEY: *Update New York! See if they lost altitude on that plane altogether.*

Watson places a call to civilian controllers at New York Center.

WATSON: *Yes, ma'am. Did you just hear the information regarding the World Trade Center?*

NEW YORK CENTER: *No.*

WATSON: *Being hit by an aircraft?*

NEW YORK CENTER: *I'm sorry?!*

WATSON: *Being hit by an aircraft.*

NEW YORK CENTER: *You're kidding.*

WATSON: *It's on the world news.*

In light of this news, someone asks Nasypany what to do with the fighters—the two F-15s from Otis Air National Guard Base—which have now just blasted off for New York at full afterburner to find American 11. (The flying time at full speed from Cape Cod to New York is about 10 minutes.) Pumped with adrenaline, Nasypany doesn't miss a beat.

08:52:40 NASYPANY: *Send 'em to New York City still. Continue! Go!*

NASYPANY: *This is what I got. Possible news that a 737 just hit the World Trade Center. This is a real-world. And we're trying to confirm this. Okay. Continue taking the fighters down to the New York City area, J.F.K. area, if you can. Make sure that the F.A.A. clears it—your route all the way through. Do what we gotta do, okay? Let's press with this. It looks like this guy could have hit the World Trade Center.*

"I'm not gonna stop what I initially started with scrambling Otis—getting Otis over New York City," Nasypany recalled when I played him this section of his tape. "If this is a false report, I still have my fighters where I want them to be."

Meanwhile, confusion is building on the ops floor over whether the plane that hit the tower really was American 11. Rumors that it was a small Cessna have started to circulate through the civilian air-traffic system. ID tech Rountree is on the phone with Boston Center's military liaison, Colin

Scoggins, a civilian manager, who at first seems to confirm that it was American 11 that went into the tower.

> 08:55:18 BOSTON CENTER *(Scoggins): Yeah, he crashed into the World Trade Center.*
>
> ROUNTREE: *That is the aircraft that crashed into the World Trade Center?*
>
> BOSTON CENTER *(Scoggins): Yup. Disregard the—disregard the tail number [given earlier for American 11].*
>
> ROUNTREE: *Disregard the tail number? He did crash into the World Trade Center?*
>
> BOSTON CENTER *(Scoggins): That's—that's what we believe, yes.*

But an unidentified male trooper at NEADS overhears the exchange and raises a red flag.

> 08:56:31 MALE NEADS TECH: *I never heard them say American Airlines Flight 11 hit the World Trade Center. I heard it was a civilian aircraft.*

Dooley, the ID desk's master sergeant, takes the phone from Rountree to confirm for herself, and the story veers off course …

> DOOLEY (to Boston): *Master Sergeant Dooley here. We need to have—are you giving confirmation that American 11 was the one—*
>
> BOSTON CENTER *(Scoggins): No, we're not gonna confirm that at this time. We just know an aircraft crashed in and …*
>
> DOOLEY: *You—are you—can you say—is anyone up there tracking primary on this guy still?*
>
> BOSTON CENTER *(Scoggins): No. The last [radar sighting] we have was about 15 miles east of J.F.K., or eight miles east of J.F.K. was our last primary hit. He did slow down in speed. The primary that we had, it slowed down below— around to 300 knots.*
>
> DOOLEY: *And then you lost 'em?*
>
> BOSTON CENTER *(Scoggins): Yeah, and then we lost 'em.*

The problem, Scoggins told me later, was that American Airlines refused to confirm for several hours that its plane had hit the tower. This lack of confirmation caused uncertainty that would be compounded in a very big way as the attack continued. (Though airlines have their own means of monitoring the location of their planes and communicating with their pilots, they routinely go into information lockdown in a crisis.)

Amid the chaos, Nasypany notices that some of his people are beginning to panic, so he makes a joke to relieve the tension.

08:57:11 NASYPANY: *Think we put the exercise on the hold. What do you think?* [Laughter.]

Just at that moment, in one of the dark, U-shaped air-traffic-control areas at New York Center, on Long Island, a half-dozen civilian controllers are watching a second plane that's turned off course: United 175, also scheduled from Boston to Los Angeles. As the controllers try to hail the pilots, a manager comes running in and confirms that the plane that hit the first tower was, indeed, a commercial airliner, rather than a small Cessna. It's just at that moment that United 175, 38 minutes into its flight and now near Allentown, Pennsylvania, moving southwest farther and farther off course, makes a sudden swing northeast toward Manhattan. Suddenly—instinctively—the civilian controllers know: it's another hijacking, and it's not going to land.

The controllers start speculating what the hijacker is aiming at—one guesses the Statue of Liberty—and the room erupts in profanity and horror. One controller is looking at his scope, calling out the rate of descent every 12 seconds as he watches the radar refresh. It is not until the last second, literally, that anyone from New York Center thinks to update NEADS. ID tech Rountree fields the call.

09:03:17 ROUNTREE: *They have a second possible hijack!*

Almost simultaneously, United 175 slams into the south tower of the World Trade Center, something several NEADS personnel witness live on CNN, including Colonel Marr, the commanding officer. (Dooley told me she remembers looking up toward the Battle Cab and, for a long moment, seeing Marr's jaw drop and everyone around him frozen.)

On the ops floor, there is considerable confusion as to whether the second hijacking New York Center just called in is the same plane that hit the second tower, or whether there are now three missing planes.

09:03:52 NASYPANY (to Marr): *Sir, we got—we've got unconfirmed second hit from another aircraft. Fighters are south of—just south of Long Island, sir. Right now. Fighters are south of Long Island.*

There's seemingly enough commotion in the Battle Cab that Nasypany needs to clarify: "*Our* fighters ..." The two F-15s, scrambled from Otis, are now approaching the city.

In the background, several troops can be heard trying to make sense of what's happening.

09:04:50—*Is this explosion part of that that we're lookin' at now on TV?*

—*Yes.*

—*Jesus …*

—*And there's a possible second hijack also—a United Airlines …*

—*Two planes?…*

—*Get the fuck out …*

—*I think this is a damn input, to be honest.*

The last line—"I think this is a damn input"—is a reference to the exercise, meaning a simulations input. It's either gallows humor or wishful thinking. From the tape, it's hard to tell.

"WE'VE ALREADY HAD TWO. WHY NOT MORE?"

Meanwhile, flying southwest over the ocean, the two fighters from Otis Air National Guard Base are streaking toward Manhattan. The pilots are startled, to say the least, when they see billowing smoke appear on the horizon; no one's briefed them about what's going on. They were scrambled simply to intercept and escort American 11—a possible hijacking—and that is all they know.

"From 100 miles away at least, we could see the fire and the smoke blowing," Major Dan Nash, one of the F-15 pilots, told me. "Obviously, anybody watching CNN had a better idea of what was going on. We were not told anything. It was to the point where we were flying supersonic towards New York and the controller came on and said, 'A second airplane has hit the World Trade Center.' … My first thought was 'What happened to American 11?'"

With both towers now in flames, Nasypany wants the fighters over Manhattan immediately, but the weapons techs get "pushback" from civilian F.A.A. controllers, who have final authority over the fighters as long as they are in civilian airspace. The F.A.A. controllers are afraid of fast-moving fighters colliding with a passenger plane, of which there are hundreds in the area, still flying normal routes—the morning's unprecedented order to ground all civilian aircraft has not yet been given. To Nasypany, the fact that so many planes are still in the sky is all the more reason to get the fighters close. ("We've already had two," he told me, referring to the hijackings. "Why not more?")

The fighters are initially directed to a holding area just off the coast, near Long Island.

Nasypany isn't happy, and he makes sure that's duly noted for posterity as he calls out to Major Fox, the leader of the Weapons Team.

09:07:20 NASYPANY: *Okay, Foxy. Plug in. I want to make sure this is on tape.... This is what—this is what I foresee that we probably need to do. We need to talk to F.A.A. We need to tell 'em if this stuff's gonna keep on going, we need to take those fighters on and then put 'em over Manhattan, Okay? That's the best thing. That's the best play right now. So, coordinate with the F.A.A. Tell 'em if there's more out there, which we don't know, let's get 'em over Manhattan. At least we got some kinda play.*

He tells the Battle Cab he wants Fox to launch two more fighters from Langley Air Force Base, in Virginia, to establish a greater presence over New York, but the request is refused. The order from the Battle Cab is to put the Langley jets on battle stations only—to be ready, but not to launch.

"The problem there would have been I'd have all my fighters in the air at the same time, which means they'd all run out of gas at the same time," Marr later explained.

Incredibly, Marr has only four armed fighters at his disposal to defend about a quarter of the continental United States. Massive cutbacks at the close of the Cold War reduced NORAD's arsenal of fighters from some 60 battle-ready jets to just 14 across the entire country. (Under different commands, the military generally maintains several hundred unarmed fighter jets for training in the continental U.S.) Only four of NORAD's planes belong to NEADS and are thus anywhere close to Manhattan—the two from Otis, now circling above the ocean off Long Island, and the two in Virginia at Langley.

Nasypany starts walking up and down the floor, asking all his section heads and weapons techs if they are prepared to shoot down a civilian airliner if need be, but he's jumping the gun: he doesn't have the authority to order a shootdown, nor does Marr or Arnold, or Vice President Cheney, for that matter. The order will need to come from President Bush, who has only just learned of the attack at a photo op in Florida.

On the ops floor, you hear Nasypany firmly pressing the issue. He briefs Marr on the armaments on board the F-15s, and how he sees best to use them "if need be":

9:19:44 NASYPANY: *My recommendation, if we have to take anybody out, large aircraft, we use AIM-9s in the face.... If need be.*

If there's another hijacking and the jets can engage, Nasypany is telling Marr, a missile fired into the nose of the plane will have the greatest chance of bringing it down.

But the prospect soon becomes real. Mo Dooley's voice erupts from the ID station on the operations floor.

9:21:37 DOOLEY: *Another hijack! It's headed towards Washington!*

NASYPANY: Shit! *Give me a location.*

UNIDENTIFIED MALE: *Okay. Third aircraft—hijacked—heading toward Washington.*

This report, received from Colin Scoggins at Boston Center, will set off a major escalation in the military response to the attack, resulting in the launch of additional armed fighter jets. But 20 months later, when the military presents to the 9/11 commission what is supposed to be a full accounting of the day, omitted from the official time line is any mention of this reported hijacking and the fevered chase it engenders.

It was the Friday before Memorial Day weekend, 2003, and the hearing room in the Hart Senate Office Building, in Washington, was half empty as the group of mostly retired military brass arranged themselves at the witness table before the 9/11 commission. The story the NORAD officers had come to tell before the commission was a relatively humbling one, a point underscored by the questions commission chairman Thomas Kean introduced during his opening remarks: How did the hijackers defeat the system, and why couldn't we stop them? These were important questions. Nearly two years after the attack, the Internet was rife with questions and conspiracy theories about 9/11—in particular, where were the fighters? Could they have physically gotten to any of the hijacked planes? And did they shoot down the final flight, United 93, which ended up in a Pennsylvania field?

On hand, dressed in business suits (with the exception of Major General Craig McKinley, whose two stars twinkled on either epaulet), were Major General Larry Arnold (retired), who had been on the other end of the secure line with NEADS's Colonel Marr throughout the attack, and Colonel Alan Scott (retired), who had been with Arnold at NORAD's continental command in Florida on 9/11 and who worked closely with Marr in preparing the military's time line. None of the military men were placed under oath.

Their story, in a nutshell, was one of being caught off guard initially, then very quickly ramping up to battle status—in position, and in possession of enough situational awareness to defend the country, and the capital in particular, before United 93, the fourth hijacked plane, would have reached Washington.

Major General Arnold explained to the commission that the military had been tracking United 93 and the fighters were in position if United 93 had threatened Washington. "It was our intent to intercept United Flight 93," Arnold testified. "I was personally anxious to see what 93 was going to do, and our intent was to intercept it."

Colonel Marr, the commanding officer at NEADS on 9/11, had made similar comments to ABC News for its one-year-anniversary special on the attacks, saying that the pilots had been warned they might have to intercept United 93, and stop it if necessary: "And we of course passed that on to the pilots: United Airlines Flight 93 will not be allowed to reach Washington, D.C."

When I interviewed him recently, Marr recalled a conversation he had had with Arnold in the heat of the attack. "I remember the words out of General Arnold's mouth, or at least as I remember them, were 'We will take lives in the air to save lives on the ground.'" In actuality, they'd never get that chance.

In the chronology presented to the 9/11 commission, Colonel Scott put the time NORAD was first notified about United 93 at 9:16 a.m., from which time, he said, commanders tracked the flight closely. (It crashed at 10:03 a.m.) If it had indeed been necessary to "take lives in the air" with United 93, or any incoming flight to Washington, the two armed fighters from Langley Air Force Base in Virginia would have been the ones called upon to carry out the shootdown. In Colonel Scott's account, those jets were given the order to launch at 9:24, within seconds of NEADS's receiving the F.A.A.'s report of the possible hijacking of American 77, the plane that would ultimately hit the Pentagon. This time line suggests the system was starting to work:

the F.A.A. reports a hijacking, and the military reacts instantaneously. Launching after the report of American 77 would, in theory, have put the fighters in the air and in position over Washington in plenty of time to react to United 93.

In testimony a few minutes later, however, General Arnold added an unexpected twist: "We launched the aircraft out of Langley to put them over top of Washington, D.C., not in response to American Airlines 77, but really to put them in position in case United 93 were to head that way."

How strange, John Azzarello, a former prosecutor and one of the commission's staff members, thought. "I remember being at the hearing in '03 and wondering why they didn't seem to have their stories straight. That struck me as odd."

The ears of another staff member, Miles Kara, perked up as well. "I said to myself, That's not right," the retired colonel, a former army intelligence officer, told me. Kara had seen the radar re-creations of the fighters' routes. "We knew something was odd, but we didn't have enough specificity to know how odd."

As the tapes reveal in stark detail, parts of Scott's and Arnold's testimony were misleading, and others simply false. At 9:16 a.m., when Arnold and Marr had supposedly begun their tracking of United 93, the plane had not yet been hijacked. In fact, NEADS wouldn't get word about United 93 for another 51 minutes. And while NORAD commanders did, indeed, order the Langley fighters to scramble at 9:24, as Scott and Arnold testified, it was not in response to the hijacking of American 77 or United 93. Rather, they were chasing a ghost. NEADS was entering the most chaotic period of the morning.

"CHASE THIS GUY DOWN"

At 9:21 a.m., just before Dooley's alert about a third hijacked plane headed for Washington, NEADS is in the eye of the storm—a period of relative calm in which, for the moment, there are no reports of additional hijackings.

The call that sets off the latest alarm ("Another hijack! It's headed towards Washington!") comes from Boston and is wholly confounding: according to Scoggins, the Boston manager, American 11, the plane they believed was the first one to hit the World Trade Center, is actually still flying—still hijacked—and now heading straight for D.C. Whatever hit the first tower, it wasn't American 11.

The chase is on for what will turn out to be a phantom plane.

9:21:50 NASYPANY: *Okay. American Airlines is still airborne—11, the first guy. He's heading towards Washington. Okay, I think we need to scramble Langley right now. And I'm—I'm gonna take the fighters from Otis and try to chase this guy down if I can find him.*

Arnold and Marr approve scrambling the two planes at Langley, along with a third unarmed trainer, and Nasypany sets the launch in motion.

It's a mistake, of course. American 11 was, indeed, the plane that hit the first tower. The confusion will persist for hours, however. In Boston, it is Colin Scoggins who has made the mistaken call.

"When we phoned United [after the second tower was hit], they confirmed that United 175 was down, and I think they confirmed that within two or three minutes," Scoggins, the go-to guy at Boston Center for all things military, later told me. "With American Airlines, we could never confirm if it was down or not, so that left doubt in our minds."

An unwieldy conference call between F.A.A. centers had been established, and Scoggins was monitoring it when the word came across—from whom or where isn't clear—that American 11 was thought to be headed for Washington. Scoggins told me he thinks that the problem started with someone overheard trying to confirm from American whether American 11 was down—that somewhere in the flurry of information zipping back and forth during the conference call this transmogrified into the idea that a different plane had hit the tower, and that American 11 was still hijacked and still in the air. The plane's course, had it continued south past New York in the direction it was flying before it dipped below radar coverage, would have had it headed on a straight course toward D.C. This was all controllers were going on; they were never tracking an actual plane on the radar after losing American 11 near Manhattan, but if it had been flying low enough, the plane could have gone undetected. "After talking to a supervisor, I made the call and said [American 11] is still in the air, and it's probably somewhere over New Jersey or Delaware heading for Washington, D.C.," Scoggins told me.

Over the next quarter-hour, the fact that the fighters have been launched in response to the phantom American 11—rather than American 77 or United 93—is referred to six more times on Nasypany's channel alone. How could

Colonel Scott and General Arnold have missed it in preparing for their 9/11-commission testimony? It's a question Arnold would have to answer later, under oath.

In the middle of the attack, however, the hijackers' sabotaging of the planes' beacons has thrown such a wrench into efforts to track them that it all seems plausible.

9:23:15 ANDERSON: *They're probably not squawking anything [broadcasting a beacon code] anyway. I mean, obviously these guys are in the cockpit.*

NASYPANY: *These guys are smart.*

UNIDENTIFIED MALE: *Yeah, they knew exactly what they wanted to do.*

Another officer asks Nasypany the obvious question.

9:32:20 MAJOR JAMES ANDERSON: *Have you asked—have you asked the question what you're gonna do if we actually find this guy? Are we gonna shoot him down if they got passengers on board? Have they talked about that?*

Approval for any such order would have to come from the commander in chief. Just after 9:30, however, the president was in his motorcade preparing to leave the Emma Booker Elementary School, in Sarasota, for the airport and the safety of Air Force One. The 9/11 commission determined that the president had not been aware of any further possible hijackings and was not yet in touch with the Pentagon.

But a clear shootdown order wouldn't have made a difference. The Langley fighters were headed the wrong way—due east, straight out to sea into a military-training airspace called Whiskey 386, rather than toward Washington, which NEADS believed was under attack. According to the 9/11 commission, the Langley pilots were never briefed by anyone at their base about why they were being scrambled, so, despite having been given the order from NEADS to fly to Washington, the pilots ended up following their normal training flight plan out to sea—a flight plan dating from the Cold War. As one pilot later told the commission, "I reverted to the Russian threat—I'm thinking cruise-missile threat from the sea."

At NEADS, a 28-year-old staff sergeant named William Huckabone, staring at his Green Eye, is the first to notice that the Langley jets are off course. His voice is a mix of stress and dread as he and the controller next to him, Master Sergeant Steve Citino, order a navy air-traffic controller who's handling the fighters to get them turned around toward Baltimore to try to cut off the phantom American 11. The navy air-traffic controller seems not to understand the urgency of the situation.

> 9:34:12 NAVY A.T.C.: *You've got [the fighters] moving east in airspace. Now you want 'em to go to Baltimore?*
>
> HUCKABONE: *Yes, sir. We're not gonna take 'em in Whiskey 386 [military training airspace over the ocean].*
>
> NAVY A.T.C.: *Okay, once he goes to Baltimore, what are we supposed to do?*
>
> HUCKABONE: *Have him contact us on auxiliary frequency 2-3-4 decimal 6. Instead of taking handoffs to us and us handing 'em back, just tell Center they've got to go to Baltimore.*
>
> NAVY A.T.C.: *All right, man. Stand by. We'll get back to you.*
>
> CITINO: *What do you mean, "We'll get back to you"? Just do it!*
>
> HUCKABONE: *I'm gonna choke that guy!*
>
> CITINO: *Be very professional, Huck.*
>
> HUCKABONE: *Okay*
>
> CITINO: *All right, Huck. Let's get our act together here.*

All hell is breaking loose around them. Boston Center has called in with *another* suspected hijacking—the controllers there don't know the call sign yet—and ID tech Watson is speed-dialing everyone she can to find a position on the resurrected American 11. In the course of a call to Washington Center, the operations manager there has sprung new information about yet another lost airplane: American 77.

> 9:34:01 WASHINGTON CENTER: *Now, let me tell you this. I—I'll—we've been looking. We're—also lost American 77—*
>
> WATSON: *American 77?*
>
> DOOLEY: *American 77's lost—*
>
> WATSON: *Where was it proposed to head, sir?*
>
> WASHINGTON CENTER: *Okay, he was going to L.A. also—*
>
> WATSON: *From where, sir?*
>
> WASHINGTON CENTER: *I think he was from Boston also. Now let me tell you this story here. Indianapolis Center was working this guy—*
>
> WATSON: *What guy?*

WASHINGTON CENTER: *American 77, at flight level 3-5-0 [35,000 feet]. However, they lost radar with him. They lost contact with him. They lost everything. And they don't have any idea where he is or what happened.*

This is a full 10 minutes later than the time Major General Arnold and Colonel Scott would give in their testimony; reality was a lot messier. Forty minutes prior, at 8:54 a.m., controllers at Indianapolis Center had lost radar contact with American 77, flying from Washington Dulles to LAX, and assumed the plane had crashed because they weren't aware of the attack in New York. Though they soon realized this was another hijacking and sent warnings up the F.A.A. chain, no one called the military; it was only by chance that NEADS's Watson got the information in her call to Washington Center.

As Watson takes in the information from Washington Center, Rountree's phone is ringing again. By this point, the other ID techs have taken to calling Rountree "the bearer of death and destruction" because it seems every time she picks up the phone there's another hijacking. And so it is again. At Boston Center, Colin Scoggins has spotted a low-flying airliner six miles southeast of the White House.

9:35:41 ROUNTREE: *Huntress* [call sign for NEADS] *ID, Rountree, can I help you?*

BOSTON CENTER *(Scoggins)*: *Latest report, [low-flying] aircraft six miles southeast of the White House.*

ROUNTREE: *Six miles southeast of the White House?*

BOSTON CENTER *(Scoggins)*: *Yup. East—he's moving away?*

ROUNTREE: *Southeast from the White House.*

BOSTON CENTER *(Scoggins)*: *Air—aircraft is moving away.*

ROUNTREE: *Moving away from the White House?*

BOSTON CENTER *(Scoggins)*: *Yeah....*

ROUNTREE: *Deviating away. You don't have a type aircraft, you don't know who he is—*

BOSTON CENTER *(Scoggins)*: *Nothing, nothing. We're over here in Boston so I have no clue. That—hopefully somebody in Washington would have better—information for you.*

This will turn out to be American 77, but since the hijackers turned the beacon off on this plane as well, no one will realize that until later. Depending on how you count, NEADS now has three reported possible hijackings from Boston (the phantom American 11 and two unidentified planes), as well as Washington Center's report that American 77 is lost.

Of these four vague and ultimately overlapping reports, the latest—word of a plane six miles from the White House—is the most urgent. The news sets off a frenzy.

> 9:36:23 NASYPANY: *Okay, Foxy [Major Fox, the Weapons Team head]. I got a aircraft six miles east of the White House! Get your fighters there as soon as possible!*
>
> MALE VOICE: *That came from Boston?*
>
> HUCKABONE: *We're gonna turn and burn it—crank it up—*
>
> MALE TECH: *Six miles!*
>
> HUCKABONE: *All right, here we go. This is what we're gonna do—*
>
> NASYPANY: *We've got an aircraft deviating eight [sic] miles east of the White House right now.*
>
> FOX: *Do you want us to declare A.F.I.O. [emergency military control of the fighters] and run 'em straight in there?*
>
> NASYPANY: *Take 'em and run 'em to the White House.*
>
> FOX: *Go directly to Washington.*
>
> CITINO: *We're going direct D.C. with my guys [Langley fighters]? Okay. Okay.*
>
> HUCKABONE: *Ma'am, we are going A.F.I.O. right now with Quit 2-5 [the Langley fighters]. They are going direct Washington.*
>
> NAVY A.T.C.: *Quit 2-5, we're handing 'em off to Center right now.*
>
> HUCKABONE: *Ma'am, we need to expedite that right now. We've gotta contact them on 2-3-4-6.*

"Six miles south, or west, or east of the White House is—it's seconds [away]," Nasypany told me later. "Airliners traveling at 400-plus knots, it's nothing. It's seconds away from that location."

The White House, then, is in immediate danger. Radar analysis in the following weeks will show that the plane abruptly veers away and turns toward the Pentagon, though the controllers at NEADS have no way of knowing this in the moment. Looking in the general capital area, one of the tracker techs thinks he spots the plane on radar, then just as quickly loses it.

9:37:56 MALE TECH: *Right here, right here, right here. I got him. I got him.*

NASYPANY: *We just lost track. Get a Z-point [coordinate] on that.... Okay, we got guys lookin' at 'em. Hold on.... Where's Langley at? Where are the fighters?*

The fighters have no chance. They're about 150 miles away, according to radar analysis done later. Even at top speed—and even if they know the problem is suicide hijackings of commercial airliners rather than Russian missiles—it will take them roughly 10 minutes to get to the Pentagon.

9:38:50 NASYPANY: *We need to get those back up there—I don't care how many windows you break!... Goddammit! Okay. Push 'em back!*

But the Pentagon is already in flames, American 77 having plowed through the E-ring of the west side of the building seconds before, at 9:37:46. The Langley fighters will not be established over Washington for another 20 minutes.

"YOU WERE JUST SO MAD"

On the ops floor, everyone is staring at CNN on the overhead screen. Seeing the first pictures of the Pentagon in flames is gut-wrenching. Nasypany's voice can be heard cursing in frustration: "Goddammit! I can't even protect my N.C.A. [National Capital Area]." You hear troops prod one another to stay focused.

CITINO: *Okay—let's watch our guys, Huck. Not the TV.*

"The more it went on, the more unbelievable it got, and then the one that did the Pentagon," Dooley told me, "we just couldn't believe it. You were just so mad that you couldn't stop these guys and so you're looking for the next one. Where are they going next?"

It looks like Washington again. Three minutes after the Pentagon is hit, Scoggins, at Boston Center, is back on the phone. The Boston controllers are now tracking Delta 1989—Boston to Las Vegas—which fits the same profile as the other hijackings: cross-country, out of Boston, lots of fuel, and possibly off course. But this one's different from the others in one key respect: the plane's beacon code is still working. In this chase, NEADS will have a chance, as the excitement in Dooley's last line reflects:

9:40:57 ROUNTREE: *Delta 89, that's the hijack. They think it's possible hijack.*

DOOLEY: *Fuck!*

ROUNTREE: *South of Cleveland. We have a code on him now.*

DOOLEY: *Good. Pick it up! Find it!*

MALE TECH: *Delta what?*

ROUNTREE: *Eight nine—a Boeing 767.*

DOOLEY: *Fuck, another one—*

They quickly find the plane on radar—it's just south of Toledo—and begin alerting other F.A.A. centers. They're not sure where the plane is headed. If it's Chicago, they're in big trouble, because they don't have any planes close enough to cut it off. Marr and Nasypany order troops to call Air National Guard bases in that area to see if anyone can launch fighters. A base in Selfridge, Michigan, offers up two unarmed fighters that are already flying, on their way back from a training mission.

9:54:54 SELFRIDGE FLIGHT OFFICER: *Here—here's what we can do. At a minimum, we can keep our guys airborne. I mean, they don't have—they don't have any guns or missiles or anything on board. But we—*

NEADS TECH: *It's a presence, though.*

But NEADS is victim again to an increasingly long information lag. Even before Rountree gets the urgent call that Delta 1989 is hijacked, a civilian air-traffic controller in Cleveland in contact with the pilot has determined that the flight is fine—that Delta 1989 isn't a hijacking after all.

Meanwhile, however, NEADS has gotten a call from a NORAD unit in Canada with yet another suspected hijacking headed south across the border toward Washington. In the barrage of information and misinformation, it becomes increasingly difficult for the controllers to keep count of how many suspected hijackings are pending. So far, it is known that three have hit buildings, but given the uncertainty about the fates of American 11 and American 77—no one knows yet that this is the plane that hit the Pentagon—the sense at NEADS is that there are possibly three hijacked jets still out there, and who knows how many more yet to be reported. At this point, no one on the military side is aware that United 93 has been hijacked.

Then, over a crackly radio, one of the Langley fighter pilots, now in a combat air patrol over Washington, is calling in urgently.

10:07:08 PILOT: *Baltimore is saying something about an aircraft over the White House. Any words?*

CITINO: *Negative. Stand by. Do you copy that, SD [Major Fox]? Center said there's an aircraft over the White House. Any words?*

FOX: *M.C.C. [Nasypany], we've got an aircraft reported over the White House.*

A fourth hijacking? Nasypany, who's running full throttle, replies instinctively.

NASYPANY: *Intercept!*

FOX: *Intercept!*

NASYPANY: *Intercept and divert that aircraft away from there.*

On one channel, you hear a weapons tech very dramatically hailing the fighters and ordering the intercept.

CITINO: *Quit 2-5 [Langley fighters], mission is intercept aircraft over White House. Use F.A.A. for guidance.*

FOX: *Divert the aircraft away from the White House. Intercept and divert it.*

CITINO: *Quit 2-5, divert the aircraft from the White House.*

PILOT: *Divert the aircraft....*

Meanwhile, Nasypany calls the Battle Cab. With a plane headed straight for the White House, Nasypany needs an update on his rules of engagement—fast.

10:07:39 NASYPANY: *Do you hear that? That aircraft over the White House. What's the word? ... Intercept and what else? ... Aircraft over the White House.*

The "what else?" is the big question: do they have the authority to shoot? The request skips up the chain to Arnold.

"I was in Vietnam," Arnold later told me. "When people are shooting at you, you don't know when it's going to stop. And that same thought went through my mind [on 9/11]. You begin to wonder, How can I get control of this situation? When can we as a military get control of this situation?"

Arnold, in turn, passes the request for rules of engagement farther up the chain.

It is in the middle of this, simultaneously, that the first call comes in about United 93. ID tech Watson fields it.

10:07:16 CLEVELAND CENTER: *We got a United 93 out here. Are you aware of that?*

WATSON: *United 93?*

CLEVELAND CENTER: *That has a bomb on board.*

WATSON: *A bomb on board?! And this is confirmed? You have a [beacon code], sir?*

CLEVELAND CENTER: *No, we lost his transponder.*

The information is shouted out to Nasypany.

NASYPANY: *Gimme the call sign. Gimme the whole nine yards.... Let's get some info, real quick. They got a bomb?*

But by the time NEADS gets the report of a bomb on United 93, everyone on board is already dead. Following the passengers' counterattack, the plane crashed in a field in Pennsylvania at 10:03 a.m., 4 minutes before Cleveland Center notified NEADS, and a full 35 minutes after a Cleveland Center controller, a veteran named John Werth, first suspected something was wrong with the flight. At 9:28, Werth actually heard the guttural sounds of the cockpit struggle over the radio as the hijackers attacked the pilots.

Werth's suspicions about United 93 were passed quickly up the F.A.A.'s chain of command, so how is it that no one from the agency alerted NEADS for more than half an hour?

A former senior executive at the F.A.A., speaking to me on the condition that I not identify him by name, tried to explain. "Our whole procedures prior to 9/11 were that you turned everything [regarding a hijacking] over to the F.B.I.," he said, reiterating that hijackers had never actually flown airplanes; it was expected that they'd land and make demands. "There were absolutely no shootdown protocols at all. The F.A.A. had nothing to do with whether they were going to shoot anybody down. We had no protocols or rules of engagement."

In his bunker under the White House, Vice President Cheney was not notified about United 93 until 10:02—only one minute before the airliner impacted the ground. Yet it was with dark bravado that the vice president and others in the Bush administration would later recount sober deliberations about the prospect of shooting down United 93. "Very, very tough decision, and the president understood the magnitude of that decision," Bush's then chief of staff, Andrew Card, told ABC News.

Cheney echoed, "The significance of saying to a pilot that you are authorized to shoot down a plane full of Americans is, a, you know, it's an order that had never been given before." And it wasn't on 9/11, either.

President Bush would finally grant commanders the *authority* to give that order at 10:18, which—though no one knew it at the time—was 15 minutes after the attack was over.

But comments such as those above were repeated by other administration and military figures in the weeks and months following 9/11, forging the notion that only the passengers' counterattack against their hijackers prevented an inevitable shootdown of United 93 (and convincing conspiracy theorists that the government did, indeed, secretly shoot it down). The recordings tell a different story, and not only because United 93 had crashed before anyone in the military chain of command even knew it had been hijacked.

At what feels on the tapes like the moment of truth, what comes back down the chain of command, instead of clearance to fire, is a resounding sense of caution. Despite the fact that NEADS believes there may be as many as five suspected hijacked aircraft still in the air at this point—one from Canada, the new one bearing down fast on Washington, the phantom American 11, Delta 1989, and United 93—the answer to Nasypany's question about rules of engagement comes back in no uncertain terms, as you hear him relay to the ops floor.

10:10:31 NASYPANY *(to floor): Negative. Negative clearance to shoot.... Goddammit!...*

FOX: *I'm not really worried about code words at this point.*

NASYPANY: *Fuck the code words. That's perishable information. Negative clearance to fire.* ID. Type. Tail.

The orders from higher headquarters are to identify by aircraft type and tail number, and nothing more. Those orders—and the fact that the pilots have no clearance to shoot—are reiterated by NEADS controllers as a dramatic chase towards the White House continues. Two more problems emerge: the controllers can't find the White House on their dated equipment, and they have trouble communicating with the Langley fighters (which are referred to by their call signs, Quit 2-5 and Quit 2-6).

CITINO: *Quit 2-6, Huntress. How far is the—suspect aircraft?*

PILOT: *Standby. Standby.... About 15 miles, Huntress.*

CITINO: *Huntress copies two-two miles.*

PILOT: *15 miles, Huntress.*

CITINO: *15 miles. One-five ... noise level please ... It's got to be low. Quit 2-6, when able say altitude of the aircraft.... Did we get a Z-track [coordinates] up for the White House?*

HUCKABONE: *They're workin' on it.*

CITINO: *Okay. Hey, what's this Bravo 0-0-5 [unidentified target]?*

FOX: *We're trying to get the Z-point. We're trying to find it.*

HUCKABONE: *I don't even know where the White House is.*

CITINO: *Whatever it is, it's very low. It's probably a helicopter.*

MALE VOICE: *It's probably the helicopter you're watching there.... There's probably one flying over the [Pentagon].*

MALE VOICE: *It's probably the smoke. The building's smoked. [They're seeing more pictures of the flaming Pentagon on CNN.]*

HUCKABONE: *Holy shit.... Holy shit ...*

CITINO: *Yes. We saw that. Okay—let's watch our guys, Huck. Not the TV.... Quit 2-6, status? SD, they're too low. I can't talk to 'em. They're too low. I can't talk to 'em.*

FOX: *Negative clearance to fire.*

CITINO: *Okay. I told 'em mission is ID and that was it.*

FOX: *Do whatever you need to divert. They are not cleared to fire.*

As it turns out, it's just as well the pilots are not cleared to shoot. Delta 1989 and the Canadian scare turn out to be false alarms. American 11 and United 93 are already down. And the fast-moving target near the White House that the armed fighters are racing to intercept turns out to be a friendly—a mistake by a civilian controller who was unaware of the military's scrambles, as weapons techs Huckabone and Citino, and their senior director, Fox, suddenly realize.

HUCKABONE: *It was our guys [the fighters from Langley].*

CITINO: *Yup. It was our guys they saw. It was our guys they saw—Center saw.*

FOX: *New York did the same thing....*

CITINO: *Okay, Huck. That was cool. We intercepted our own guys.*

At that point in the morning, Marr later told me, preventing an accidental shootdown was a paramount concern. "What you don't want happening is a pilot having to make that decision in the heat of the moment where he is bearing all that burden as to whether I should shoot something down or not," Marr said.

It is 12 minutes after United 93 actually crashed when NEADS's Watson first hears the word. Her voice is initially full of hope as she mistakenly believes she is being told that United 93 has landed safely.

10:15:00 WATSON: *United nine three, have you got information on that yet?*

WASHINGTON CENTER: *Yeah, he's down.*

WATSON: *What—he's down?*

WASHINGTON CENTER: *Yes.*

WATSON: *When did he land? Because we have confirmation—*

WASHINGTON CENTER: *He did—he did—he did not land.*

Here, on the tape, you hear the air rush out of Watson's voice.

WATSON: *Oh, he's down* down?

MALE VOICE: *Yes. Yeah, somewhere up northeast of Camp David.*

WATSON: *Northeast of Camp David.*

WASHINGTON CENTER: *That's the—that's the last report. They don't know exactly where.*

"I KNOW WHAT SPIN IS"

On June 17, 2004, a year after the 9/11 commission's initial public hearing, Major General Arnold and a more robust contingent of NORAD and Pentagon brass arrived to testify before the commission at its 12th and final public meeting. This time, they would testify under oath.

The hearing began with an elaborate multi-media presentation in which John Farmer Jr., the commission's senior counsel, John Azzarello, and another staff attorney, Dana Hyde, took turns illustrating, in withering detail, the lag time between when the F.A.A. found out about each of the hijacked aircraft and the time anyone from the agency notified the military. Excerpts from the NEADS tapes and parallel recordings from the F.A.A., which show the civilian side in equal turmoil, were played in public for the first time. (Both sets of recordings were provided to the commission only after being subpoenaed.)

The focus of the pointed questioning that followed wasn't on why the military didn't do better, but rather on why the story Major General Arnold and Colonel Scott had told at the first hearing was so wrong, in particular with respect to the phantom American 11, which the officers had never mentioned, and United 93, which they claimed to have been tracking. Commissioner Richard Ben-Veniste, who cut his teeth 30 years earlier working for the Watergate special prosecutor, led off the questioning and came out swinging.

"General, is it not a fact that the failure to call our attention to the miscommunication and the notion of a phantom Flight 11 continuing from New York City south in fact skewed the whole reporting of 9/11?" he asked Arnold, who replied that he had not been aware of those facts when he testified the year before.

"I've been in government and I know what spin is," Farmer, the senior counsel, told me. The military's story was "a whole different order of magnitude than spin. It simply wasn't true." Farmer says he doesn't understand why the military felt the need to spin at all. "The information they got [from the F.A.A.] was bad information, but they reacted in a way that you would have wanted them to. The calls Marr and Nasypany made were the right ones."

Both Marr and Arnold bristled when I asked about the commission's suspicion that there had been an effort to spin the story. "I can't think of any incentive why we'd want to spin that," Marr said, his eyes tensing for the first time in what had been friendly interviews. "I'll be the first to admit that immediately after—in fact, for a long time after—we were very confused with who was what and where, what reports were coming in. I think with having 29 different reports of hijackings nationwide, for us it was next to impossible to try and get back there and figure out the fidelity [about the morning's chronology] that the 9/11 commission ended up being able to show."

Azzarello, Farmer, and several other commission members I spoke to dismissed this fog-of-war excuse and pointed out that not only had the military already reviewed the tapes but that the false story it told at the first hearing had a clear purpose. "How good would it have looked for the government in general if we still couldn't have stopped the fourth plane an hour and 35 minutes [into the attack]?" Azzarello asked. "How good would it have looked if there was a total breakdown in communication and nothing worked right?"

If nothing else, it might have given the public a more realistic sense of the limitations, particularly in the face of suicide terrorism, of what is, without doubt, the most powerful military in the world.

As one of its last acts before disbanding, in July 2004, the 9/11 commission made referrals to the inspector general's offices of both the Department of Transportation (which includes the F.A.A.) and the Defense Department to further investigate whether witnesses had lied. "Commission staff believes that there is significant evidence that the false statements made to the commission were deliberately false," Farmer wrote to me in an e-mail summarizing the commission's referral. "The false testimony served a purpose: to obscure mistakes on the part of the F.A.A. and the military, and to overstate the readiness of the military to intercept and, if necessary, shoot down UAL 93." A spokesman for the Transportation Department's inspector general's office told me that the investigation had been completed, but he wasn't at liberty to share the findings, because the report had not been finalized. A spokesman at the Pentagon's inspector general's office said its investigation had also been completed, but the results are classified.

Poring over time-stamped transcripts that undercut the Pentagon's official story, one is tempted to get caught up in a game of "gotcha." For those on the operations floor in the thick of it that day, however, the cold revelations of hindsight are a bitter pill to swallow.

Listening to the tapes, you hear that inside NEADS there was no sense that the attack was over with the crash of United 93; instead, the alarms go on and on. False reports of hijackings, and real responses, continue well into the afternoon, though civilian air-traffic controllers had managed to clear the skies of all commercial and private aircraft by just after 12 p.m. The fighter pilots over New York and D.C. (and later Boston and Chicago) would spend hours darting around their respective skylines intercepting hundreds of aircraft they deemed suspicious. Meanwhile, Arnold, Marr, and Nasypany were launching as many additional fighters as they could, placing some 300 armed jets in protective orbits over every major American city by the following morning. No one at NEADS would go home until late on the night of the 11th, and then only for a few hours of sleep.

Five years after the attack, the controversy around United 93 clearly eats at Arnold, Marr, Nasypany, and several other military people I spoke with, who resent both conspiracy theories that accuse them of shooting the flight down and the 9/11 commission's conclusion that they were chasing ghosts and never stood a chance of intercepting any of the real hijackings. "I don't know about time lines and stuff like that," Nasypany, who is now a lieutenant colonel, said in one of our last conversations. "I knew where 93 was. I don't care what [the commission says]. I mean, I care, but—I made that assessment to put my fighters over Washington. Ninety-three was on its way in. I knew there was another one out there. I knew there was somebody else coming in—whatever you want to call it. And I knew what I was going to have to end up doing." When you listen to the tapes, it couldn't feel more horrendously true.

When I asked Nasypany about the conspiracy theories—the people who believe that he, or someone like him, secretly ordered the shootdown of United 93 and covered it up—the corners of his mouth began to quiver. Then, I think to the surprise of both of us, he suddenly put his head in his hands and cried. "Flight 93 was not shot down," he said when he finally looked up. "The individuals on that aircraft, the passengers, they actually took the aircraft down. Because of what those people did, I didn't have to do anything."

On the day, however, there was no time for sentiment. Within 30 seconds of the report that United 93 has crashed, killing everyone on board, once again, the phone is ringing.

10:15:30 POWELL: *Southeast just called. There's another possible hijack in our area....*

NASYPANY: *All right.* Fuck ...

REVIEW

MARTIN AMIS

ALL THAT SURVIVES IS LOVE

At 8.21 the first plane, American 11, turned off its transponder (the automatic tracking device); then it changed course and began its descent. The air traffic controllers were still trying to locate American 11 when word came through that "a light plane" had hit the World Trade Centre. On CNN the controllers see the site of the crash. The wound in the building's side is in the shape of a plane: not a Cessna or a twin-prop but what they call a "heavy"—a Boeing 757.

In the real-time docudrama *United 93,* we see the second plane strike its target, not on CNN, but with the naked eye. What appears to be the original footage, startlingly, has been placed within a vast vista of morning blue. Our POV is the control post at Newark International.

By now the North Tower, to the right, is like a demonic smokestack, giving off a leaning column of furry black fumes. As United 175 impends, the controllers gasp at its velocity. Mohamed Atta's incision, in the North Tower, will now look surgically discreet—compared to the kinetic ecstasy sought by Marwan al Shehhi.

United 175 was travelling at nearly 600mph, a speed that the 767 was not designed to reach, let alone sustain. This happened eleven seconds and three minutes after nine o'clock—the core moment of September 11. Now they knew. And so did the passengers on United 93.

That plane, too, was travelling at 580mph when it crashed, nose first and upside down, forming a crater 175 feet deep in an empty field near Shanksville, Pennsylvania. Of the 3,000 who died on that day, only those

---

This review originally appeared in the *London Times* on June 1, 2006. Copyright © Times Newspapers Limited 2006. Reprinted by permission.

on board the fourth plane had no doubts about the fate intended for them. The director of *United 93,* Paul Greengrass, is right: they were "the first people to inhabit the post 9/11 world." We may strongly identify with one passenger, an earnest Scandinavian, who cannot accept the new reality: he argues for full co-operation with the hijackers, hoping, one assumes, for a leisurely siege on some North African tarmac. The others know, from cellphones and airphones, that it isn't going to be like that.

They rise up, and the plane comes down.

At this point, 106 minutes in and with only seconds to go, you will find yourself, I am confident, in a state of near-perfect distress—a distress that knows no blindspots. *The New York Times* called *United 93* "the feel-bad movie of the year."

But this hardly covers it. The distress is something you can taste, like a cud, returned from the stomach for further mastication: the ancient flavour of death and defeat. Your mind will cast about for a molecule, an atom of consolation. And what you will reach for is what they reached for. Like the victims on the other three planes, but unlike them, because they knew, the passengers called their families and said that they loved them. It is an extraordinary validation, or fulfilment, of Larkin's lines at the end of "An Arundel Tomb":

> ...To prove Our almost-instinct almost true:
> What will survive of us is love.

A Hollywoodised version of the story would begin with Bruce Willis, in the part of Todd Beamer ("Let's roll"), waking in Manhattan, and languidly reminding his wife that he is off to San Francisco on an early flight from Newark. *United 93* begins with the desolate, self-hypnotising drone of early-morning prayer. In their budget hotel room the four hijackers, wearing clean white vests, are aspiring to the murderous serenity urged on them by their handlers in Afghanistan.

Soon they are among the passengers and are being processed to the gate. We are in the familiar, and suddenly painful, everyday: the spotty young woman with her laptop; the shared travel anxiety of an elderly couple; the grunt of relief from a panting young man, pleased, as you would be, to get there just in time. And it is here, in the departure bay, that Greengrass makes his one major divergence from the known: Ziad Jarrah, the pilot and leader (and literally a different breed from the "muscle" Saudis), says six words into his mobile phone—"I love you. I love you."

Greengrass may have other sources. According to a footnote in the 9/11 Commission Report, Jarrah did make a final call to his fiancée, Aysel Senguen; but he called her from the hotel, and she described their conversation as brief and not unusual.

Thus the moment in the departure bay, though broadly justifiable, is hugely anomalous, and for this reason: it is artistic. And elsewhere, while Greengrass cannot banish his talents of eye and ear, he refuses, quite rightly, to be artistic. Those six words hang in the air, and are balanced and answered by the tearful protestations of the doomed passengers. In this reading, Jarrah, too, knew what would survive of him.

What is not in doubt is that Jarrah loved Aysel Senguen. He is, by many magnitudes, the least repulsive of the 19 killers of September 11, 2001. An affluent Lebanese, he left the beaches and discos of Beirut at the age of 21, in 1996, and went to Germany to study dentistry (he later switched to aeronautics).

There he met and fell in love with Aysel Senguen, the student daughter of a Turkish immigrant. He was human in other ways. Defying cell policy, he stayed close to his family, and made several returns to the bedside of his ailing father in Lebanon. Most centrally, he had doubts, and needed to be cajoled and rallied right to the end. And all this is there in the extraordinary performance of Khalid Abdalla. There are no weak points, and no obtrusively strong points, in the *United 93* ensemble. But among the little-knowns and the unknowns and the people playing themselves, Abdalla, perhaps destabilisingly for the movie, is something like its star. His history is all held in, yet it is all there in his suffering eyes.

At Newark International there was a routine—indeed wholly predictable—delay on the ground, caused by weight of traffic. Those 42 minutes changed everything. If United had left on time, there would have been no passenger revolt. Instead, there would have been horror at the White House or horror at the Capitol.

Osama bin Laden wanted the White House. Mohamed Atta, the operational leader, vaguely argued that the approach would be too difficult, and wanted the Capitol.

Interestingly, the President was not in the White House (he was puzzling his way through *My Pet Goat* in Sarasota, Florida), but the President's wife might well have been in the Capitol (pushing No Child Left Behind). In any case, both buildings were evacuated by 9.30—two minutes after the hijack of United 93.

Greengrass peels off, at punctual intervals, to follow the traffic controllers (whose efforts were highly impressive) and to follow the military (whose efforts were pitiable); but by now the other three planes have crashed, and the focus is all on United 93. Sickening suspense about the revolt of the terrorists is replaced, thereafter, by sickening suspense about the revolt of the passengers. In the aftermath of that day, a CIA official noted that, even though the state spent $40 billion a year on internal security, all that stood between America and September 11 was "a bunch of rugby players." But America didn't even have that.

There is no bunch, no pack, of rugby players. There is one huge athlete who spearheads the charge (with a marvellously giddy, drunken expression on his face); but he leads a motley band—they are just passengers, after all. The countercoup is rendered in strict accordance with Greengrass's method. There is no final pow-wow, there are no husky valedictions. It simply erupts, with desperate suddenness, and they are coming down the aisle with their weapons—kitchen knives, wine bottles, boiling water.

And they didn't really have a chance. This was one of the existential nightmares of United 93. They were up in the sky at maximum throttle in a huge machine. But no one on board knew how to land it. Not Jarrah, who was trained only for level flight. By now the passengers are using the drinks cart as a battering-ram, and Jarrah, lover of Aysel Senguen, is doing what he can to make the plane yaw, then pitch, then dive. These are the last words on the black box, translated from the Arabic, each and every one utterly futile, and utterly meaningless. "Allah is the greatest! Allah is the greatest! Is that it? I mean, shall we put it down?" "Yes, put it in it, and pull it down." We can say, at least, that the passengers saved America from a fourth scar on its psyche. And there is that glimmer of double meaning in the film's title. And that is all.

Greengrass doesn't spare us—but he is able to spare us something. When was the last time you boarded an aeroplane that had no children in it? United 93 was evidently such a flight. And if it hadn't been? It is hard to defend your imagination from such a possibility. "What's happening? You see, my child, the men with the bloodstained knives think that if they kill themselves, and all of us, they will go at once to a paradise of women and wine." No, I suppose you would just tell him or her that you loved them, and he or she would tell you that they loved you too. Love is an abstract noun, something nebulous. And yet love turns out to be the only part of us that is solid, as the world turns upside down and the screen goes black. We can't tell if it will survive us. But we can be sure that it's the last thing to go.

REVIEW

Peter Bradshaw

What other subject is there? What other event is there?

Nothing is so important, so inextinguishably mind-boggling as the terrorist kamikaze flights of 9/11. Al-Qaida gave the world a situationist spectacle that dwarfed anything from the conventional workshops of politics and culture. Since then, Hollywood has indirectly registered tremors from Ground Zero, but here is the first feature film to tackle the terrible day head on, and Paul Greengrass has delivered a blazingly powerful and gripping recreation of the fourth abortive hijacking. It is conceived in a docu-style similar to *Bloody Sunday,* his movie about the 1972 civil rights march in Northern Ireland. He does not use stars or recognisable faces, and many of the characters in the air traffic control scenes are played by the actual participants themselves.

This is an Anti-Titanic for the multiplexes—a real-life disaster movie with no Leo and Kate and no survivors: only terrorists whose emotional lives are relentlessly blank, and heroes with no backstory. Greengrass reconstructs the story of the hijacked plane that failed to reach its target (the Capitol dome in Washington DC) almost certainly owing to a desperate uprising by the passengers themselves, who were aware of the WTC crashes from mobile phone-calls home, and who finally stormed the cabin, where terrorists were flying the plane. With unbearable, claustrophobic severity, Greengrass keeps most of his final act inside the aircraft itself.

The director is able to exploit the remarkable fact that the sequence of events, from the first plane crashing into the World Trade Centre at a quarter to nine, to the fourth plane ditching into a field in Shanksville, Pennsylvania, at three minutes past 10, fits with horrible irony inside conventional

---

This review originally appeared in *The Guardian* on June 2, 2006. Copyright © 2006 by Guardian News and Media Limited. Reprinted by permission.

feature-film length, and he is able to unfold the story in real time. It is at this point that a critic might wish to say: caution, spoilers ahead. But we all know, or think we know, how the story of *United 93* comes out, and this is what makes the film such a gutwrenching example of ordeal cinema. When the lights go down, your heart-rate will inexorably start to climb. After about half an hour I was having difficulty breathing. I wasn't the only one. The whole row I was in sounded like an outing of emphysema patients.

Every last tiny detail is drenched with unbearable tension, especially at the very beginning. Every gesture, every look, every innocent greeting, every puzzled exchange of glances over the air-traffic scopes, every panicky call between the civil air authority and the military—it is all amplified, deafeningly, in pure meaning. And the first scenes in which the United 93 passengers enter the plane for their dull, routine early-morning flight are almost unwatchable. These passengers are quite unlike the cross-section of America much mocked in *Airplane!*—with the singing nun and the cute kid—neither are they vividly drawn individuals with ingeniously imagined present or future interconnections, like the cast of TV's *Lost*. They are just affluent professionals from pretty much the same caste, with no great interest in each other, and nothing in common except their fate. And all these people are ghosts, all of them dead men and dead women walking. When they are politely asked to pay attention to the "safety" procedures, ordinary pre-9/11 reality all but snaps in two under the weight of historical irony.

But what does happen at the end of the story? In his memorial address, President Bush implied that the passengers committed an act of tragic self-immolation, rather than see the Capitol destroyed. Is that what happened? Greengrass evidently disagrees. In his vision, the passengers have a quixotic idea of using one passenger, a trained pilot, to wrest control and bring the plane down safely to the ground—a Hollywood ending, perhaps. But there is something very un-Hollywood in Greengrass's refusal to confirm that without the passengers' action they would have hit the Capitol. On the contrary, his script shows the terrorists making a miscalculation of their own.

United 93 is growing, in popular legend, into the tragic and redemptive part of the 9/11 story: America's act of Sobibor defiance. It is a myth-making which is growing in parallel with jabbering conspiracy theories that the plane was shot down by US air-force jets and the whole passenger-action story is a cover-up. On that latter point, Greengrass's movie shows us that it is easy to be wise after the event; it is a reminder of how unthinkable 9/11 was, of how all too likely it was that the civil and military authorities would not have mobilised in time, and that any action would indeed have to come from the passengers themselves. The film is at any rate fiercely critical of Bush and Cheney, who are shown being quite unreachable by the authorities, desperate for leadership and guidance.

United 93 does not offer the political or analytical dimension of Antonia Bird and Ronan Bennett's 9/11 docu-drama *Hamburg Cell*; there is no analysis or explanation. The movie just lives inside that stunned, astonished 90 minutes of horror between one epoch and the next—and there is, to my mind, an overwhelming dramatic justification for simply attempting to face, directly, the terrible moment itself. The film might, I suspect, have to be viewed through an obtuse fog of punditry from those who feel that it is insufficiently anti-Bush. It shouldn't matter. Paul Greengrass and his cinematographer Barry Ackroyd have created an intestinally powerful and magnificent memorial to the passengers of that doomed flight. It is the film of the year. I needed to lie down in a darkened room afterwards. So will you.

REVIEW

DAVID DENBY

"No one is going to help us. We've got to do it ourselves." Those plain, unarousing words, spoken by a man ordinary in looks but remarkable in perception and courage, are a turning point in *United 93,* Paul Greengrass's stunning account of how a group of airline passengers, almost certain of death, decided on the morning of September 11th to fight back against hijackers on a suicide mission. But Greengrass doesn't build the moment as a turning point in any conventional way. The words of the anonymous passenger, a round-faced man who has been studying the hijackers ever since they made their first moves, are spoken firmly but without emphasis, and no dead air is placed around the statement to give it extra weight. The hijackers have taken over the flight at knifepoint and murdered a passenger in first class, and everyone else, appalled, has gathered at the back of the plane. By this time, both the passengers and the crew understand what is going on. Many of them have spoken by cellphone to friends and relatives, and they know that the World Trade Center and the Pentagon have been hit. The hijackers aren't going to land and hold them hostage; they are going to slam them into another building. The only issue—for the flight controllers and the military people we see at other points in the movie, as well as for the people on board—is what can be done to take control of a situation both terrifying and unprecedented. Greengrass's movie is tightly wrapped, minutely drawn, and, no matter how frightening, superbly precise. In comparison with past Hollywood treatments of Everyman heroism in time of war, such as Hitchcock's hammy *Lifeboat,* or more recent spectacles, like *War of the Worlds,* there's no visual or verbal rhetoric, no swelling awareness of the Menace We All Face. Those movies were guaranteed to raise a lump in our throats. In this retelling of actual

---

This review appeared in the May 1, 2006, issue of *The New Yorker*. Reprinted by permission.

events, most of our emotion is centered in the pit of the stomach. The accumulated dread and grief get released when some of the male passengers, shortly after those few words are spoken, rush the hijackers stationed at the front of the plane with the engorged fury of water breaking through a dam.

A fair amount of distaste for this movie has been building in recent weeks. Would the heroic event—which ended when the plane crashed in Pennsylvania, killing everyone aboard—be exploited in some way? And why do we need to take this death trip? But *United 93* is a tremendous experience of fear, bewilderment, and resolution, and, when you replay the movie in your head afterward, you are likely to think that Greengrass made all the right choices. Born in England in 1955, he has directed, among other films, *Bloody Sunday,* a re-creation of the British Army's massacre of Northern Irish protesters, in 1972; and *The Bourne Supremacy,* a franchise action movie in which a near-silent Matt Damon tears up Europe. What unites all three films is a dynamic use of the camera. It's handheld and thrust into the tumult, yet somehow—and this is the essence of Greengrass's art—we see what we need to see.

The movie begins slowly, with the morning prayers of the sweet-faced young men who will become the terrorists; the drowsy routine at Newark airport, where Flight 93, bound for San Francisco, began; the passengers amiably settling into the plane; the puzzlement at the Federal Aviation Administration command center, as first one and then another flight veers off course. When Flight 93 is hijacked, the passengers initially respond with panic, while the flight controllers on the ground, burning through their disbelief, try (without success) to rouse the military. Steadily, the editing becomes quicker, the language grows more terse and peremptory, and we begin to pick up details in a flash, out of a corner of the camera's eye.

The hijackers kill the pilots, but Greengrass doesn't show us their deaths; we just see their bodies being dragged across the cockpit, from the point of view of a flight attendant in the middle of the plane. Rejecting standard front-and-center staging, Greengrass works in half-understood fragments. When the passengers revolt, the violence is not an artfully edited fake but a chaotic, flailing scramble, and it's not performed by charismatic types displaying their prowess. In a story of collective and anonymous heroism, we don't want Denzel Washington leading the charge or Gene Hackman wrathfully telling the military to get on the stick. Greengrass uses real flight attendants, air controllers, and pilots, and mixes them in with little-known or unknown actors. As an ensemble, the players are stolid, but in a good way—they exhibit a combination of incomprehension and intelligence, befuddlement and alertness, that feels right. They live within the moment without overdefining it.

Flight 93's departure, scheduled for 8 a.m., was delayed. By the time the plane got off the ground, the attacks on the World Trade Center were only a few minutes away. In the movie, once the flight is aloft Greengrass sticks to real time, and the passing minutes have an almost demonic urgency. This is true existential filmmaking: there is only the next instant, and the one after that, and what are you going to do? Many films whip up tension with cunning and manipulation. As far as possible, this movie plays it straight. A few people made extraordinary use of those tormented minutes, and *United 93* fully honors what was original and spontaneous and brave in their refusal to go quietly.

Review

Stephen King

Ready or Not

I'm a fast feeler but a slow thinker, so it took me a while to figure out why the reviews of *United 93* left me feeling angry. Especially considering the fact that they were almost entirely positive, and I agreed with them—I think it is a shoo-in for a Best Picture nod at Oscar time. I'll go even further. Now, more than five weeks after seeing it on the day it opened, I think it's one to put on the same shelf with *The Godfather*. The reviews don't reflect that, of course—film critics rarely go so far—but the groundwork is there. In preparation for this piece, I read through nearly three dozen reviews and came across few discouraging words. Not even on the blogs, where, as a rule, the self-appointed critics eat their young.

My feeling coalesced into thought when I read the title of Jack Mathews' review in the *New York Daily News*: "Excellent but Unbearable." Near the end, Mathews says, "...you can certainly question the point of making a movie that...leaves us with the same sickening mix of loss and anger we felt at the time."

With that remark in mind, I went through the reviews again and found that all but two or three raised the question of whether or not it was still "too soon" to make a movie about the events of 9/11. Most concluded that it wasn't, but advised caution on the part of would-be viewers (extreme caution in some cases, it seemed to me). Reading those notices again, in this light, helped me understand why I was so angry: Those reviews infantilize the American public.

Well, to a large extent that's been going on for a long time—eat your veg-

---

Copyright © 2006 by Stephen King. Reprinted by permission of Stephen King c/o Ralph M. Vicinanza, Ltd. Originally published in *Entertainment Weekly* on June 9, 2006.

gies, don't party too hearty, wear your bike helmet, wear your seat belt, sweetums, or Mr. Policeman gonna give you a ticket. Maybe we even need some of this, but considering that 9/11 started a war—or served as the excuse for one, depending on your political point of view—that has already cost nearly as many American lives as were lost on that September day, I think most of us over the age of 18 (and many under it) are capable of watching how the 40 doomed souls on Flight 93 behaved in their final hour. Especially since many seem to have acquitted themselves with the sort of guts and backs-to-the-wall ingenuity that Americans celebrate each July.

We're hypocritical from belly to spine when it comes to film violence, you know? When I hear critics warning audiences that *United 93* might upset them—in the same year that Eli Roth's ferocious and bloody *Hostel* topped the box office—I can only shake my head in amazement. It's enough to make a person recall Jack Nicholson in *A Few Good Men*, snarling "You can't handle the truth!"

The don't-wake-the-baby signs are all there, and not just from film critics who wanted Mr. and Mrs. Average Moviegoer to know what they'd be getting into with *United 93*. There is the current administration's effort to manage combat footage from Iraq (what combat footage?) and their effort to ban any coverage of returning flag-draped coffins. They don't want us to look; they feel we might be disturbed; they think we're not quite ready. After being seriously wounded by a roadside bomb north of Baghdad, ABC News anchor Bob Woodruff effectively became a nonperson. Kimberly Dozier of CBS, injured as part of a news crew that got blown up in Baghdad (with two crew members dead), has been sighted once. In a way, her lone sighting sums the whole deal up: It consisted basically of Army personnel, looking like pallbearers, surrounding what appeared to be nothing but tubes and monitors. The woman herself had disappeared. Did I want to view her pain, her wounds? God, no. But she deserved more than the bureaucracy gave her (and us): She's doing as well as expected, okay? Now go and look at something nice. How about Robin Williams in *RV*?

But there's more upsetting stuff in the pipeline, possibly including Oliver Stone's big-budget *World Trade Center*. It seems clear that this painful subject has spurred at least one director—Paul Greengrass—to the best work of his life. It may well do the same for Oliver Stone, a great filmmaker on those occasions (*JFK* was not one of them; *Platoon* was) when he cares to remove his head from his ass. But remember that the bottom line in Hollywood is the buck. Hollywood will be watching closely to see if America can "handle the truth!" Maybe that isn't the way it should be, but it's the way it has to be in a society that doesn't subsidize its film industry.

Subsidized or not, Hollywood has a powerful voice, and it will holler "Look at this! See this! Think about this!"... as long as people are brave enough to look, see, think, and pay for the experience. It's clear from the reviews that a lot of critics think the moviegoing public is too scared to do that when it comes to 9/11. Scared of pretty much everything, in fact, but fake blood and rubber monsters.

One of the few critics who didn't raise the "Is America ready?" question was *Entertainment Weekly*'s Lisa Schwarzbaum. She asked a better one, I think: Do we need to see this? The philosopher George Santayana, who died almost 50 years before 9/11, had the answer to that one: "Those who cannot remember the past are condemned to repeat it."

UNITED AIRLINES FLIGHT 93'S CREW AND PASSENGERS

Flight 93 - Crew

Captain Jason M. Dahl
First Officer LeRoy Homer
Lorraine G. Bay, Flight Attendant
Sandra Bradshaw, Flight Attendant
Wanda Anita Green, Flight Attendant
CeeCee Lyles, Flight Attendant
Deborah Welsh, Flight Attendant

Flight 93 – Passengers

Christian Adams
Todd Beamer
Alan Anthony Beaven
Mark Bingham
Deora Frances Bodley
Marion R. Britton
Thomas E. Burnett, Jr.
William Joseph Cashman
Georgine Rose Corrigan
Patricia Cushing
Joseph DeLuca
Patrick Joseph Driscoll
Edward P. Felt
Jane Folger
Colleen Fraser
Andrew Garcia
Jeremy Glick
Kristin White Gould
Lauren Catuzzi Grandcolas
Donald Freeman Greene
Linda Gronlund
Richard Guadagno
Toshiya Kuge
Hilda Marcin
Waleska Martinez
Nicole Carol Miller
Louis J. Nacke, II
Donald Peterson
Jean Hoadley Peterson
Mark Rothenberg
Christine Snyder
John Talignani
Honor Elizabeth Wainio

ABOUT THE FLIGHT 93 NATIONAL MEMORIAL

On September 24, 2002, Congress passed the Flight 93 National Memorial Act. The Act created a new national park unit to "commemorate the passengers and crew of Flight 93 who, on September 11, 2001, courageously gave their lives, thereby thwarting a planned attack on our Nation's Capital." The memorial will be developed near Shanksville, Pennsylvania, where Flight 93 crashed on September 11, 2001.

When completed, Flight 93 National Memorial will encompass 2,200 acres, almost 1,300 acres of which will be dedicated to the design features, and 900 acres will be protected through partnerships with local residents and groups.

The Flight 93 National Memorial project is making history as the first national park designed entirely through an open, public competition. The yearlong, international competition received more than 1,000 submissions created by professionals and members of the general public. The National Park Service is the steward of the Flight 93 National Memorial.

The final design selection for the Flight 93 National Memorial (announced September 7, 2005) was created by Paul Murdoch Architects, a Los Angeles–based firm. A diverse jury comprised of family members, community representatives and design professionals chose the winning design because it most completely exemplifies the mission statement for the memorial. This mission statement grew out of hundreds of responses to a public survey and countless hours of discussion by families of the passengers and crew, community residents, national experts and National Park Service staff.

The Flight 93 National Memorial's mission statement is "A common field one day. A field of honor forever. May all who visit this place remember the collective acts of courage and sacrifice of the passengers and crew, revere this hallowed ground as the final resting place of those heroes, and reflect on the power of individuals who choose to make a difference."

To find out more or to make a contribution to the Flight 93 Memorial Fund, please visit **www.honorflight93.org**.

CAST AND CREW CREDITS

UNIVERSAL PICTURES and STUDIOCANAL
Present
In association with SIDNEY KIMMEL ENTERTAINMENT
A WORKING TITLE Production
A PAUL GREENGRASS Film

"UNITED 93"

Casting by AMANDA MACKEY CSA CATHY SANDRICH GELFOND CSA JOHN HUBBARD DAN HUBBARD	Costume Designer DINAH COLLIN Production Designer DOMINIC WATKINS	Executive Producers DEBRA HAYWARD LIZA CHASIN Produced by TIM BEVAN
Music by JOHN POWELL	Editors CLARE DOUGLAS CHRISTOPHER ROUSE ACE	ERIC FELLNER LLOYD LEVIN PAUL GREENGRASS
Line Producer MAIRI BETT	Director of Photography BARRY ACKROYD BSC	Written and Directed by PAUL GREENGRASS

CAST

Flight 93 - Crew
Captain Jason M. Dahl . . . . JJ JOHNSON
First Officer LeRoy Homer
. . . . GARY COMMOCK
Deborah Welsh . . . . . . POLLY ADAMS
CeeCee Lyles . . . . OPAL ALLADIN
Wanda Anita Green . STARLA BENFORD
Sandra Bradshaw . . . . . TRISH GATES
Lorraine G. Bay . . . NANCY McDONIEL

Flight 93 - Passengers
Todd Beamer . . . DAVID ALAN BASCHE
William Joseph Cashman
. . . . RICHARD BEKINS
Jane Folger . . . . SUSAN BLOMMAERT
Joseph DeLuca . . . . RAY CHARLESON
Thomas E. Burnett, Jr.
. . . . . . CHRISTIAN CLEMENSON
Waleska Martinez . LIZA COLON-ZAYAS
Linda Gronlund . . . . . LORNA DALLAS
Colleen Fraser . . . . . . DENNY DILLON
Deora Frances Bodley . . TRIESTE DUNN
Lauren Catuzzi Grandcolas
. . . . . . KATE JENNINGS GRANT
Jeremy Glick . . . . . PETER HERMANN
Kristin White Gould . . . . TARA HUGO
Georgine Rose Corrigan
. . . . MARCELINE HUGOT
Mark Bingham . . CHEYENNE JACKSON
John Talignani . . . . JOE JAMROG
Louis J. Nacke, II . . . COREY JOHNSON
Toshiya Kuge. . . . . . MASATO KAMO
Jean Hoadley Peterson . BECKY LONDON
Andrew Garcia. . . . PETER MARINKER
Marion R. Britton
. . . . . JODIE LYNNE McCLINTOCK
Hilda Marcin . . . . LIBBY MORRIS
Donald Peterson . . . . TOM O'ROURKE
Alan Anthony Beaven . . SIMON POLAND
Donald Freeman Greene . . DAVID RASCHE
Christian Adams . . . . ERICH REDMAN
Patrick Joseph Driscoll
. . . . MICHAEL J. REYNOLDS
Edward P. Felt . . . . . JOHN ROTHMAN
Richard Guadagno. . . . . DANIEL SAULI
Patricia Cushing . . . REBECCA SCHULL
Honor Elizabeth Wainio . CHLOE SIRENE
Nicole Carol Miller . . . OLIVIA THIRLBY
Mark Rothenberg . . . . . . CHIP ZIEN
Christine Snyder. . LEIGH ZIMMERMAN

Flight 93 – Hijackers
Ziad Jarrah. . . . . . . KHALID ABDALLA
Saeed Al Ghamdi . . . LEWIS ALSAMARI
Ahmed Al Haznawi . OMAR BERDOUNI
Ahmed Al Nami . . . . JAMIE HARDING

Boston Air Traffic Control
Boston 3 . . . . MICHAEL BENCAL
Boston 5 . . . . TOM FITZGERALD
Boston 6 . . . . BARD MARQUES
Supervisor . . . . JOHN MORAITIS
Boston 4. . . . . . . THOMAS ROBERTS
Boston Controller 5 . . . SCOTT TOURIN

Cleveland Air Traffic Control
Cleveland Supervisor . . AMANDA BOXER
Cleveland Supervisor . MORGAN DEARE
Cleveland Controller . . DANIEL FRASER

Herndon
Ben Sliney . . . . AS HIMSELF
Tobin Miller . . . . AS HIMSELF
Rich Sullivan . . . . AS HIMSELF
Tony Smith . . . . AS HIMSELF
John White . . . MICHAEL BOFSHEVER
Herndon 1 . . . . CAROL BENTO
Herndon 3 . . . . ROBERT SERVISS
Herndon 2 . . . . MATT SIEBERT
Herndon 5 . . . . PETER WONG

NEADS
Major James Fox . . . . AS HIMSELF
1st Lt. Jeremy Powell . . . . . AS HIMSELF
Senior ID Tech
. . . . STAFF SGT. SHAWNA FOX
Major Kevin Nasypany
. . . . PATRICK ST. ESPRIT
Colonel Robert Marr . . GREGG HENRY

New York Air Traffic Control
Paul Thumser . . . . . PETER PELLICANI
NYC 1 . . . . CURT APPLEGATE
NYC 5 . . . . KEVIN DELANEY
NYC 2 . . . . JOHN KAPLUN
New York Controller . . . JOHN E. SMITH

Newark Tower
Greg Callahan . . . . AS HIMSELF
Rick Tepper . . . . AS HIMSELF
Newark Supervisor . . . . . BILL WALSH

Stunts . . . . ABBI COLLINS
NICK CHOPPING
KELLY DENT
DAVE FISHER
AMANDA FOSTER
SARAH FRANZL
PAUL HERBERT
ROWLEY IRLAM
PAUL KENNINGTON
JAMIE MILLINGTON
DANIEL NAPROUS
RAY NICHOLAS
BRIAN NICKELS
PETER PEDRERO
ALISON RYAN
GORDON SEED
CC SMIFF
ROY TAYLOR

CREW
Written and Directed by
. . . . PAUL GREENGRASS
Produced by . . . . TIM BEVAN
ERIC FELLNER
LLOYD LEVIN
PAUL GREENGRASS
Executive Producers . DEBRA HAYWARD
LIZA CHASIN
Director of Photography
. . . . BARRY ACKROYD BSC
Editors . . . . CLARE DOUGLAS
CHRISTOPHER ROUSE ACE
RICHARD PEARSON
Production Designer
. . . . DOMINIC WATKINS
Costume Designer . . . . DINAH COLLIN
Visual Effects Supervisor
. . . . PETER CHIANG
Associate Producers
. . . . MICHAEL BRONNER
KATE SOLOMON
Line Producer . . . . MAIRI BETT
Post-Production Supervisor
. . . . MIKE SOLINGER
Music by . . . . JOHN POWELL
Sound Mixer . . . . CHRIS MUNRO
Casting by . . . . AMANDA MACKEY CSA
CATHY SANDRICH GELFOND CSA
JOHN HUBBARD
DAN HUBBARD
SIG De MIGUEL
Production Manager . . . SASHA HARRIS
First Assistant Director
. . . . CHRIS CARRERAS
Hair & Makeup Designer
. . . . KIRSTIN CHALMERS
'A' Camera Operator . . KLEMENS BECKER
Production Accountant . . JIM HAJICOSTA
Script Supervisor . . . . LIZ WEST
Supervising Art Director . . ALAN GILMORE
Set Decorator . . . MICHAEL STANDISH
Stunt Coordinator . . . . GREG POWELL

Supervising Sound Editors
. . . . OLIVER TARNEY MPSE
EDDY JOSEPH MPSE

FOR WORKING TITLE

Chief Operating Officer
. . . . ANGELA MORRISON
Executive in Charge of Production
. . . . MICHELLE WRIGHT
Head of Legal & Business Affairs
. . . . SHEERAZ SHAH
Production Executive
. . . . SARAH-JANE ROBINSON
Music Supervisor . . . . . . NICK ANGEL
Chief Financial Officer
. . . . SHEFALI GHOSH
Senior Legal & Business Affairs Executive
. . . . GRÁINNE McKENNA
Legal & Business Affairs Executive
. . . . LUCY WAINWRIGHT
Executive Coordinator. . . . ANN LYNCH
Assistant Production Coordinator
. . . . KATE BAILEY
Assistant to Tim Bevan
. . . . CHLOÉ DORIGAN
Assistant to Eric Fellner . . . ALIZA JAMES
Music Coordinator . . ALEXANDRA HILL
Production Coordinator
. . . . SAM KNOX-JOHNSTON
Second Assistant Director. . SALLIE HARD
Third Assistant Director
. . . . TOM BREWSTER
Assistant Production Coordinator
. . . . HOLLIE FOSTER
Assistant to Mr. Greengrass
. . . . ANDREA TRUSCOTT
Production Assistant . MIKE CLARK-HALL
Assistant to the Cast . . . SUZIE BATTERS
Production Runner
. . . . JAMES CHESTERTON
Floor Runners. . . . . SANDRINE LOISY
JAE-SUNG OH
ADAM BYLES
CELENA RADWANSKI
JACK BREWSTER
SAM HAVELAND
First Assistant 'A' Camera
. . . . BEBE DIERKEN
Second Assistant 'A' Camera
. . . . NICOLE DIERKEN
Grip 'A' Camera . . . JOHN McSWEENEY
Central Loader . . . . TIM MORRIS
First Assistant 'B' Camera
. . . . CARL HUDSON
Second Assistant 'B' Camera
. . . . SARA DEANE
Grip 'B' Camera . . . . . ANDY EDRIDGE
Libra Head Operator . . . DAVE FREETH
Crane Operator . . . ANDY THOMSPSON
FT2 Camera Trainee . . CHRIS McALEESE
FT2 Grip Trainee
. . . . ANTHONY BENJAMIN
Video Playback Operators
. . . . ADRIAN SPANNA
Sound Maintenance . . . COLIN WOODS
Second Boom Op . . NATHAN DUNCAN
Sound Engineer . . . . JIM McBRIDE
First Assistant Accountants
. . . . JASON POTTER
ROB SEAGER
Cashier . . . . LAWRENCE JOSEPH
Post Production Coordinator
. . . . JOYLON HAVERSON
Location Manager . . . KEITH HATCHER
Assistant Location Manager
. . . . PAUL LANGFORD
Assembly Editors . . . TOM KINNERSLEY
CHRISTOPHER BELL
First Assistant Editor . . . . . IAN DIFFER
VFX Editor . . . . . . JO-ANNE DIXON
Second Assistant Editor
. . . . ESTHER BAILEY
Assistant Editors . . . . JAKE COOK
LAURENCE JOHNSON
ALEX FINN
Dialogue Editors . RICHARD FORDHAM
TONY CURRIE
SIMON CHASE
IAN EYRE
Sound Editors . . . . STUART MORTON
MARTIN CANTWELL
JACK WHITTAKER
Supervising Foley Editor
. . . . HARRY BARNES
Foley Editor. . . . . ALEX JOSEPH
Assistant Sound Editor . . DAVID MACKIE
Sound Editorial Support . . CAROL JONES
Sound Editorial and Post Production by
. . . . SOUNDELUX LONDON
Special Effects Consultant
. . . . JOSS WILLIAMS
Special Effects Coordinator
. . . . MIKE DAWSON
Senior SFX . . . . STUART DIGBY

SFX Crew . . . . TERRY FLOWERS
KEITH DAWSON
TONY EDWARDS

ANDREW BUNCE
HAYLEY WILLIAMS
BEN BROADBRIDGE
Costume Supervisor . . . MARION WEISE
Assistant Costume Designer
. . . . RICHARD SALE
Costume Standby . . . . LEE CROUCHER
SUE CASEY
UNA NICHOLSON
LUAN PLACKS
BARLEY MASSEY
Costume Trainee . . . . NATALIE WALSH

Key Hairdresser
. . . . . . FRANCESCA CROWDER
Hair & Make-up Artists . . LOZ SCHIAVO
DONALD McINNES
SHARON PAULA O'BRIEN
KRISTIE MATTHAIE
PETA DUNSTALL
JULIA WILLSON
RENATA GILBERT
Art Directors . . . . JOANNA FOLEY
ROMEK DELIMATA
Standby Art Director . . SARAH STUART
Production Buyer . . . . . . EMMA DAVIS
Draughtsman . . . JORDAN CROCKETT
Assistant Concept Artist
. . . . . . JONATHAN RICHARDSON
Art Department Coordinator
. . . . SALLY ROSS
Graphic Artist . . . . . . KATHY HEASER
Art Department Assistant
. . . . JAMES COLLINS
Food Stylists . . . . . . KATHERINE TIDY
MARY LUTHER

<u>Researchers & Advisors</u>
U.S. Air Traffic Control . . . BEN SLINEY
COLIN SCOGGINS
U.S. Air Force Advisors
. . . . . LT. COL. STEPHEN CLUTTER
MAJOR JAMES FOX
1ST LT. JEREMY POWELL
Religious Advisors . . . AJMAL MASOOR
MUNA AMR
KHALED HROUB
DR. MAHJOOB ZWEIRI, INSTITUTE
FOR MIDDLE EASTERN & ISLAMIC
STUDIES, DURHAM UNIVERSITY
Lebanese Advisor . . . . . INSAF DAHAM
Saudi Advisor . . . . TWAFIK SAIF
Digital Playback & Design
. . . . USEFUL COMPANIES

Creative Supervisor . . . SIMON STAINES
Project Supervisor . . . . . JUSTIN OWEN
Coordinator . . . . . SARA-JANE OWEN
Technicians . . . . . . GAVIN McKENZIE
DAVID KIRMAN
RHYS OWEN
Radar Programmer . . DANIEL GRIFFITH
Property Master . . . . RICHARD MILLS
Dressing Propsmen . . ANDREW GRANT
DON SANTOS
TOM READ
GRAHAM STICKLEY
Standby Props . . JONATHAN DOWNING
ANDREW FORREST
Property Storeman . . . . ALAN BRYANT
Drapesman . . . . CHRIS SEDDON
Construction Manager
. . . . MALCOLM ROBERTS
Standby Carpenter . . . GARRY MOORE
Standby Rigger . . . . DAVID GRAY
Supervising Carpenter
. . . . MARTIN HUBBARD
Carpenters . . . . . WAYNE HAMMOND
PAUL NOT MACAIRE
MARK BRADY
PETER MAYHEW
DAVID MAYHEW
SIMON MARJORAM
TOM McCARTHY
KEVIN DEARDON
SIMON ROBILLIARD
JO HAWTHORNE
LEIGH CHESTERS
GRAHAM WEAMES
JAMES WEAMES
GARRY FISHER
WAYNE DAY
DANIEL WELLS
Chargehand Painter . . . . ALAN GOOCH
Chargehand Scenic Painter
. . . . MICHAEL SOTHERAN
Scenic Painter . . . . . . JAY SOTHERAN
Painters . . . . JASON IVALL
MICHAEL GUNNER
Supervising Rigger . . . . . . JOHN FIELD
Riggers . . . . ROBERT GURNEY
PAUL MITCHELL
NEIL ROBERTSON
NICHOLAS ROSS
KENNETH SLATER
JOHN WRIGHT
Supervising Metal Worker . . NIGEL GRAY
Welders . . . . . STEPHAN BATTERHAM
NORRIE HENDERSON

	BRUCE MAYHEW
	ANTHONY WASS
Supervising Stagehand . . .	KEITH SMITH
Stagehands	FRANK CARR
	JOHN FOLLY
	GRAHAM JARMAN
	EDDIE O'NEILL
	LEONARD ROBERTS
	COLIN SMITH
	ROYSTON SMITH
Supervising Plasterer . .	ROBERT VOYSEY
Plasterers	STEPHEN WATTS
	OLIVER HOWLETT
Gaffer	MATT MOFFATT
Rigging Gaffer	PAT MILLER
Best Boy	VINCE MADDON
Electricians.	PETER BRIMSON
	JOHN CAMPBELL
	KEVIN DAY
	BRANDON EVANS
	WARREN EWEN
	KEVIN FITZPATRICK
	MARK HANLON
	PETER HARRIS
	BARRY McCULLAGH
	JOE McGEE
	NOEL MILLER
	KENNY MONGER
	ROB MONGER
	ROBERT O'BRIEN
	LARRY PAR
	RAYMOND POTTER
	LAURIE SHANE
	PAUL SHARP
	PAUL STEWART
Desk Operator	CHRIS CRAIG
Moving Light Rig Operator. .	ANDY JUPP
Chargehand Electrical Rigger	
. . . .	PAUL HARFORD
Electrical Riggers. .	ROBERT DIEBELIUS
	DARREN HOWTON
	IAN PAPE
	JOHN PITT
	JOHN ROBERTSON
	GRANT WIESINGER
Stunt Safety	DOMINIC PREESE
Assistant to Stunt Coordinator	
. . . .	JADE GORDON
Casting Associate	KATE BULPITT
Casting Assistant	KELLY HENDRY
Additional & Background Casting	
. . . .	2020 CASTING
Stills Photographer . .	JONATHAN OLLEY

Health & Safety Consultant	
. . . .	JHA FILM SAFE-T
Standby Health & Safety Advisor	
. . . .	CHRIS CULLUM
Unit Nurse.	CARRIE JOHNSON
Caterers	
ALL ENGLAND FILM CATERERS LTD.	
Transport Captain . .	BARRIE WILLIAMS
Driver to Mr. Greengrass	
. . . .	DAVID MANNING
Unit Driver.	DANNY JARMAN
Additional Unit Cars.	SET WHEELS
. . . .	WESTGATE CARS
Facilities Captain	
. . . .	LORENZO ROBINSON
Minibus Drivers.	GAVIN MULLINS
	ANDY CLARK

SECOND UNIT

Second Unit Director .	CHRIS FORSTER
Directors of Photography . . .	MIKE ELEY
	SEAN BOBBITT
First Assistant Director	
. . . .	ROBERT P. GRAYSON
Third Assistant Director	
. . . .	NICK SHUTTLEWORTH
First Assistant Camera. . .	DAN SHORING
Second Assistant Camera	NATASHA BACK
Clapper Loaders	FRAN WESTON
	SIMON GILMOUR
Camera Grips.	JOHN RAKE
	COLIN GINGER
	DAVID CADWALLADER
	DAVID CROSS
Script Supervisor	POLLY HOPE
Sound Mixers	IAN MUNRO
	STEVE THOMAS
Boom Op.	GARY DODKIN
Standby Props	GARY IXER
Makeup Artist	SARA RIESEL
Gaffer	JOHN ASH
Electricians	POP KEELING
	JOHN KING
Standby Rigger	STEVE HOWE
Camera Car	COLIN ELVES

NEW YORK UNIT

Unit Production Manager	
. . . .	BRYAN THOMAS
First Assistant Director . . .	JULIE BLOOM
Second Assistant Director	
. . . . . .	KIERSTEN PILAR MILLER
Second Second Assistant Director	
. . . .	MATT POWER

159

A Camera Operator	PHIL OETIKER
First Assistant A Camera	JIM BELLETIER
Second Assistant A Camera	LEE VICKERY
B Camera Operator/Steadicam	JAMIE SILVERSTEIN
First Assistant B Camera	JEFF DUTEMPLE
Second Assistant B Camera	NATE SWINGLE
Loader	TIM McNULTY
Art Director	CLEMENT PRICE-THOMAS
Art Department Coordinator	EVA RADKE
Location Manager	PEGGY ROBINSON
Production Coordinator	DREW TIDWELL
Assistant Coordinator	ANDREA PAPPAS
Production Secretary	SCOTT SULLENS
Office Production Assistants	ALEXANDER J. SMELSON, SHANNON KEARNEY
Accountant	OLIMPIA RINALDI-IODICE
Assistant Accountant	KATHERINE DeJESUS
Payroll Accountant	PATRICIA PORTER
Set Production Assistants	CHRIS RYAN, JASON BOOTHIE, BORYAN JAVINOVICH, JILLIAN ROACHE, MARK ROMANELLI, CHERIE ROSS, JAMIE WEISMAN
Video Assist	CHRISTOPHER MURPHY
Second Video Assist	MAX FRANKSTON
Wardrobe Supervisor	KATHERINE KARBOWSKI
Wardrobe Shopper	LIZ McGARRITY
On-Set Costumiers	MEI LAI HIPPISLEY COXE, AMY BURT, LAURA DOWNING, RAUL FERREIRA
Gaffer	PETR HLINOMAZ
Best Boy	JON DELGADO
Genny Op	T.Y CHENNAYULT
Electrician	DAVE SAMUELS
Key Grip	JOHN DOLAN
Additional Grip	PAT SHELBY
Dolly Grip	BRAD GOSS
Hairdresser	PATRICIA GRANDE
Makeup Artist	EVA POLYWKA
Location PA	JOSH KESNER
Prop Master	RUTH Di PASQUALE
Standby Scenic	JESSIE WALKER
Set Decorator	WILLIAM REYNOLDS
Leadman	PETER DUNBAR
Script Supervisor	SHEILA PAIGE
Sound Mixer	RICHARD A. MADER
Boom Op	JASON BENJAMIN
Sound Utility	MICHELLE MADER
Transport Captain	JIM BUCKMAN
Transport Co-Captain	BILL BAKER
Parking Coordinator	JON JOHNSON
Unit Medic	DEBORAH BLAKE
Stills Photographer	K.C. BAILEY
Extras Casting	KAREN ETCOFF
Catering	THE WILSON RIVAS COMPANY

Plate Unit

Production Coordinator	HOLLY RYMON
Assistant Coordinator	JENNIFER MADELOFF
Accountant	ANSLEM KING
Camera Operator	CHRIS NORR
First Assistant Camera	CHRIS REYNOLDS
First Assistant Camera	DIANNE KORONKIEWICZ
Second Assistant Camera	LISA ORIGLIERI
Key Grip	JOHN DOLAN
Additional Grip	PAT SHELBY
Wardrobe PA's	SARA LIBMANN, JESSICA HILLYER
Office PA	PARRY CREEDON
Location Manager – Washington	CAROL FLAISHER
Location Assistant – Washington	CHAN CLAGGETT
Sound Mixer	SERGE STANLEY
NY Teamster Driver	LANCE DeJESUS
Washington Teamster Driver	GLEN WILLIAMS

Aerial Unit

Pilot	TOM McMURTRY
Co-Pilot	MICHAEL GRAM
Camera Operator	JOHN KRONHOUSE
Technician	PETER GRAF
Loader	KEN THOMPSON

Digital Visual Effects by
.... DOUBLE NEGATIVE

Visual Effects Digital Supervisor	. . . . JOHN MOFFATT
3-D Supervisors	RICK LEARY
	STUART FARLEY
VFX Producers	MATT PLUMMER
	CLARE TINSLEY
	ALEX HOPE
Digital Artists	ABRAHAM KAM-BANOPOULOS
	ALASTAIR CRAWFORD
	AMI PATEL
	ANDRE BRIZARD
	CHRISTOPH SALZMANN
	DANIEL EVANS
	DANIEL WOOD
	DARREN CHRISTIE
	ELLIE FAUSTINO
	FOAD SHAH
	GAVIN HARRISON
	GUY WILLIAMS
	HELENA MASARD
	JAMES GUY
	JAMES TOMLINSON
	JAMIE BRIENS
	JIM STEEL
	JOHN KILSHAW
	KIRSTY LAWLOR
	MATTHEW SHAW
	NIK BROWNLEE
	PAWEL GROCHOLA
	PEDRO GARCIA
	PETE HANSON
	PETER GODDEN
	ROHIT GILL
	SANJU TRAVIS
	SEAN DANISCHEVSKY
	SHARON WARMINGTON
	SIMON HUGHES
	TIM JONES
	TOM STEADMAN
	TREVOR YOUNG
	TRISTAN MYLES
	VANESSA BOYCE
	WILL SKELLHORN
Digital Intermediate by	. . . . FRAMESTORE CFC
Colourist	ASA SHOUL
Producers	SARAH MICALLEF
	MARIA STROKA
Digital Grading Assistants	. . . . STEVE WAGENDORP
	BRIAN KRIJGSMAN
Scanning and Recording	. . . . JASON BURNETT
Digital Cleanup . . .	ANNABEL WRIGHT
Sound Re-Recorded at. . .	DE LANE LEA POST PRODUCTION LIMITED
Re-Recording Mixers .	MICHAEL PRESTWOOD SMITH
	DOUGLAS COOPER
Additional Re-Recording Sound Mixers	SVEN TAITS
	MATHEW GOUGH
	CHRIS BURDON
Foley Mixer	MARK HACKETT
Foley Artists	PAUL HANKS
	IAN WAGGOTT
Foley Recorded at .	UNIVERSAL SOUND
ADR Supervisor	PAUL CONWAY
UK ADR Mixer . . .	ANDY THOMPSON
UK ADR Facility . .	GOLDCREST POST PRODUCTION FACILITIES
New York ADR Supervisor	. . . . GINA R. ALFANO
New York ADR Mixers	. . . . DAVID BOULTON
	MARK De SIMONE
New York ADR Facilities . .	SOUNDONE
	MAGNO SOUND & VIDEO
LA ADR Supervisor	. . . . ROBERT C. JACKSON
LA ADR Mixers . . .	CHRIS NAVARRO
	RON BEDROSIAN
LA ADR Facilities . .	WILSHIRE STAGES
	TODD-AO HOLLYWOOD
ADR Voice Casting	. . . . BRENDAN DONNISON
	AND VANESSA BAKER
Digital Main and End Titles by	. . . . CINEIMAGE
Plane Hire	LEKI AVIATION
Camera Equipment	ARRI MEDIA
Lighting Equipment . .	ARRI LIGHTING
Grip Equipment	ALPHA GRIP
Moving Light Rig	. . . . . . ELSTREE LIGHT & POWER
Chapman Camera Cranes and Dollies	. . . . . P S PRODUCTION SERVICES LIMITED - CANADA
Color by	DELUX
Laboratory Contact. . . .	CLIVE NOAKES
Negative Cutting	CUTTING EDGE

Production Telecine Facilities . . . . ARION
Post Production and Telecine Facilities Stills
Processing . . . . PINEWOOD
        PHOTOGRAPHIC CENTRE
Walkie Talkies . . . . WAVEVEND
Editing Facilities & Equipment
  . . . . CLEAR CUT HIRES
Avid and Pro Tools Equipment . GEARBOX
    (SOUND AND VISION) LIMITED
Facility Vehicles . . . . TRANSLUX
Insurance . . . AON/ALBERT G. RUBEN
Legal Clearances . . MARSHALL/PLUMB
      RESEARCH ASSOCIATES, INC.
U.S. Clearances . . JENNIFER MADELOFF
Visa Services . . . . . . DORA KUMARA,
        GONZALEZ & HARRIS
Executive in Charge of Music for Universal
Pictures . . . . KATHY NELSON
Music Conducted by
  . . . . GAVIN GREENAWAY
Music Orchestrated by
  . . . . JOHN A. COLEMAN
        JOHN ASTON THOMAS
Orchestral Contractor
  . . . . ISOBEL GRIFFITHS
Orchestra Leader . . . . GAVYN WRIGHT
Music Recorded and Mixed by
  . . . . SIMON RHODES
Additional Recording . . . DAN LERNER
Recorded and Mixed at
  . . . . ABBEY ROAD, STUDIO 1
Assistant Engineer . . . . ROB HOUSTON
Music Copyist . . . . . FIESTA MEI LING
Solo Vocal . . . . OLIVER POWELL
Composer Assistants . . . GERMAINE AND
        MATTEO FRANCO

Footage Courtesy of . . . . CNN
        GETTY IMAGES
        NBC
      WORLD BACKGROUNDS

With Thanks to:
Silke Adams, Gen. Larry Arnold, Christian Basballe, Erich A. Bay, Marc Bay, David Beamer, Michelle Beamer, Peggy Beamer, Chris Beaven, John Beaven, Kimi Beaven, Sonali Beaven, Sherri Benson, Tim Benson, Bob Berger, Andrew Bernstein, Jim Best, Lyzbeth Glick Best, Kevin Bianchi, Jerry Bingham, Karen Bingham, Barbara Black, Michael Blake, Lt. Col. Kacey Blaney, Sandra Bodley, Jim Bohleber, Deborah Borza, David Bottiglia, Phil Bradshaw, Ross Bratlee, Paul Britton, Laura Brough, Laura J. Brown, Beverly Burnett, Deena Burnett, Tom Burnett Sr., Mary Jarmson Bush, Marilyn Callahan, John Carr, Maggie Cashman, Doug Church, Sam Corsello, Phil Craig, Pegeen Cushing, Sandy Dahl, Col. Dawne Deskins, Dan Diggins, MSgt. Maureen Dooley, Chris Driscoll, August Essmann, Emma Essmann, Jayne M. Essmann, Tony Farthing, Gordon Felt, Sandy Felt, Laura Folger, Lucy M. Folger, Robert T. Folger, Christine Fraser, Dorothy Garcia, Jerry Garegnani, Charles Glanville, Sheena Glanville, Donna Glessner, Emmy Glick, Pam Gould, Jack Grandcolas, Charlie Greene, Claudette Greene, Jody Greene, Randy Greene, Terry Greene, Doris Gronlund, Elsa Gronlund Strong, Beatrice Guadagno, Jerry Guadagno, Lori Guadagno, Matt Hall, John Hartling, Dan Hatlestad, Lesia Hatlestad, Mike Hayes, Bill Heiderich, Carole Heiderich, Esther Heymann, Alice A. Hoglan, Candyce Hoglan, Lee N. Hoglan, Vaughn Hoglan, Melodie Homer, Carol Hughes, Capt. Herb Hunter, Sandra Jamerson, Lisa Jefferson, Robert Jones, Donita Judge, Mariko Kaburagi, Betty Kemmerer, Mike Kucharek, Yachiyo Kuge, Kathy Kulik, Paige Lang, Diqui LaPenta, Kevin Larson, Lasham ATC, Rick Law, Bonnie LeVar, Mark Libby, Angela Lopez, Annette Lord, Barbara Lunt, Lorne Lyles, Sugar Manley, Col. Robert Marr, Marriot Langley, Catherine Miller, David Miller, Tiffney Miller DeVries, John and Judy Mulligan, Maureen Mulligan, The National Park Service, Kenny Nacke, Louis Nacke, Paula Nacke Jacobs, Col. Kevin Nasypany, Newark Airport, Andrew Newell, Carole O'Hare, Hamilton Peterson, Ian Pescaia, Pinewood Hotel, Catherine Price, Jennifer Price, Andy Prodger, Quality Hotel Langley, Renaissance Hotel Heathrow, Jeff Richardson, Steve Robuck, Bette Root, Ed Root, Edwin Root, Carrie Ross, Meredith Rothenberg, SSgt. Stacia Rountree, Eva Rupp, Capt. Mark Seal, Grace Sherwood, Janice Snyder, Neal Snyder, Col. Clark Speicher, Merry Speicher, Cathy Stefani, Wayne Stefani, Lynn Silva, Stansted Airport, Mary Steiner, John Tamm, Oliver Tobias, MSgt John Tomassi, Chris Tucker, Joan Marie Turchiano, Terry Raymond Tyksinski, Allison Vadhan, Ben Wainio, Sarah Wainio, Barbara

Welsh, Patrick Welsh, John Werth, John White, Mary Louise White, Patrick White, Craig Woythaler, Peter Zalewski, Mitch Zykofsky, Shari Zykofsky.

The filmmakers gratefully acknowledge the assistance of the Department of Defense, in particular:

Philip Strub
Department of Defense
Master Sergeant Larry A. Schneck, USAF
Department of Defense Project Officer

48th Fighter Wing, RAF Lakenheath, United Kingdom
North American Aerospace Defense Command, Peterson AFB, Colorado
Northeast Air Defense Sector, New York ANG, Rome, New York
102d Fighter Wing, Massachusetts ANG, Otis ANG Base, Massachusetts
119th Fighter Wing, North Dakota ANG, Fargo, North Dakota

Filmed on location in New York, Boston, Washington, Morocco and at Pinewood Studios, England.

This film is not a literal telling of the events of September 11, 2001 and United 93. It is a creative work based on fact, but in dramatising the story for the screen some characters have been composited or invented, certain events, dialogue and chronology have been fictionalised and of course much has been left out. No assumption should be made that any of the persons, companies or products shown or mentioned in the film have endorsed this production.

This motion picture is protected under the laws of the United States and other countries and its unauthorised duplication, distribution or exhibition may result in civil liability and criminal prosecution.

©2006 Universal Studios.
All Rights Reserved.

ABOUT THE WRITER/DIRECTOR

Paul Greengrass (Written and Directed by / Produced by) wrote and directed the critically lauded, documentary-style feature *Bloody Sunday*, about the 1972 civil rights march in Northern Ireland that resulted in thirteen deaths. *Bloody Sunday*'s awards include the Golden Bear at the Berlin Film Festival 2002, the World Cinema Audience Award at the Sundance Film Festival 2002, and Best Director, the British Independent Film Awards 2002.

He most recently directed the international blockbuster *The Bourne Supremacy*, which grossed more than $50 million during its domestic opening weekend and went on to earn more than $175 million at the U.S. box office. Greengrass' other credits include *Omagh* (Best Single Drama, BAFTA 2005), *The Murder of Stephen Lawrence* (Best Single Film, BAFTA 2000; Special Jury Prize, BANFF TV Festival 2000), *The Fix*, *The Theory of Flight* (Best Foreign Film, Brussels Film Festival 1999), and *Resurrected* (Interfilm and OCIC Jury Awards, Berlin Film Festival 1989).

Greengrass has also written and directed many documentaries, including the official Live Aid documentary, *Food, Trucks and Rock and Roll*. He began his career on *World in Action*, where he won a BAFTA. He was also co-writer with Peter Wright of the controversial bestseller *Spycatcher*.